FORMULA FOR WEALTH

Alan James

CKBooks Publishing

Publisher's Cataloging-in-Publication Data
Names: James, Alan, author.
Title: Formula for wealth / Alan James.
Description: New Glarus, WI : CKBooks Publishing, 2020.
Identifiers: ISBN 978-1-949085-34-1 (paperback) | ISBN 978-1-949085-35-8 (ebook)
Subjects: LCSH: Wealth. | Wealth--Management. | Saving and investment. | Budgets, Personal. | Finance, Personal. | BISAC: BUSINESS & ECONOMICS / Finance / Wealth Management. | BUSINESS & ECONOMICS / Personal Finance / Budgeting. | BUSINESS & ECONOMICS / Personal Finance / Investing.
Classification: LCC HB251 .J36 2020 (print) | LCC HB251 (ebook) | DDC 332.024/01--dc23.

LCCN: 2020921736
Copyright © 2020 By Alan James LLC
All rights reserved.
Published in the United States of America
Cover photograph by Filograph

CKBooks Publishing, PO Box 214, New Glarus, WI, 53508, ckbookspublishing.com

"Almost everyone wants to become richer, so what separates those with wealth from the majority who always seem to be struggling to make it to the end of each month? *Formula for Wealth* by Alan James will outline the financial and emotional constraints that are keeping your finances from growing. Divided into two sections, the guide will give you a strong foundation of how finances are built, including how to budget intelligently and how investments can open doors of financial freedom if done correctly. You will also be able to plan effectively for your retirement and any financial problems that will arise. Being wealthy has different meanings to people. So what does being wealthy mean to you? *Formula for Wealth* will show you the necessary actions you need to execute to get to the financial destination. You will then apply what you have learned as a unique blueprint to your own personal financial situation.

"*Formula for Wealth* by Alan James is an in-depth analysis of growing your wealth and maintaining it. The strategies are practical and easy to follow. The equations were very interesting and quite detailed. Even if you want to skip the mathematical equations, you will gain so much knowledge regarding increasing your finances. What separates this guide from other books on financial management is that the author delves into the psychological barriers that could be preventing you from becoming wealthy. I loved the chapter on how to increase your assets; the information was very interesting and easy to execute too.

My favorite chapter was Other Tips For Success as this gives us so many opportunities to increase our finances even further. If you are open to becoming more financially successful and are willing to take the actions outlined in this guide, then this is the perfect financial book for you."

Lesley Jones

"*Formula for Wealth* by Alan James lays the fundamental groundwork so people can gain control of their own financial well-being. It provides succinct, straight-to-the-point guidelines revolving around James' mathematical Equation of Wealth to fuel a lifelong application of wealth-building practices that can help people set and achieve their financial goals.

"Wealth is desired by many but achieved by few. In *Formula for Wealth,* Alan James gives readers the basic principles that surround wealth building and offers insights on various real-life financial vessels, which can help people grow their net worth over time. Through logical narrative coupled with visual graphs and hypothetical storytelling, James draws in readers and helps them navigate the realm of personal finance. This is not a get rich quick type of book. This is a book that can serve as a life-long guide, a financial blueprint that can help people in various stages of life take stock of what they currently have and what they can do to grow it. Financial literacy is an undervalued skill that has lifelong applications.

"*Formula for Wealth* contains all the necessary

concepts and lessons, including how to manage risk and take into account real-life scenarios that can impact one's finances. People looking to know more about how wealth is built and how to go about building it need look no further. *Formula for Wealth* is a treasure trove of information that challenges its readers to apply the knowledge it imparts and sets them on a path towards constant and consistent financial mindfulness."

Eduardo Aduna

"I believe the premise of this book and the ideas behind it are good ones. I like the concept of the equation and have no reason whatsoever to believe it isn't the groundbreaking theory that will work for so many who are desperate to eliminate debt and have the genuine security of a solid retirement."

Asher Syed

To my loving wife,
Terry

Table of Contents

Introduction

Do people really read introductions? If you do, then I'll let you know what to expect from this book.

Most people want to be wealthy, so why isn't everyone as wealthy as they could be? There are two things that could hold people back from building as much wealth as possible. Either they do not understand what it takes to build wealth, or they do not do what they know will build wealth. If you know what it would take to build wealth, wouldn't you want to do it? So then if you are not as wealthy as you would like, it must be that you would like a better understanding of how wealth is built. This book presents information on how to grow and manage wealth through narrative, explanation, math and graphs, which will provide you a strong foundation to successfully build your wealth. We have all heard of rich people that we would not have expected to be rich, such as a janitor that leaves a small fortune to charity or a librarian that gave a large amount of money to a library. There are many individual paths to wealth, but the principles are the same for all of us.

I have created a mathematical equation I call the Equation for Wealth. I use this equation to help remove any mystery about how wealth is generated. Whatever your financial goal, the Equation for Wealth will help you figure out what it will take to reach your financial goals. I will explain the mathematical Equation for Wealth and do so in a way that is easy to read and understand.

This book will do more than cover math, it will also explain practical issues related to wealth. I will blend practical matters such as budgeting and investing with the concepts of the Equation for Wealth. If you don't like math, you are welcome to jump over the equations. There are many books on the subject of either personal finance or wealth management. They are both part of the Equation for Wealth.

I will also explain what I call the Formula for Wealth. The Formula for Wealth is applying the equation to our lives, how you use the mathematical equation to generate your personal wealth. The first part of the Formula for Wealth that we will look at will involve personal finance. You cannot manage wealth until you have some wealth to manage. The next part of the Formula for Wealth will involve wealth management. We will go through practical examples of how to generate and increase wealth.

I start this book describing wealth and discussing personal finance factors and wealth management factors of the Equation for Wealth. I then begin the discussion of the Equation for Wealth. The Equation for Wealth would not be as helpful to you without an understanding of what is involved in generating wealth. My book concludes with some of the problems that interfere with making wealth and practical tips to grow your wealth.

This book will explain the Equation for Wealth and show how wealth is built. After reading this book, you will know what to do to build your wealth. Then it will be up to you to do what you need to do to become as wealthy as you can. The Equation for Wealth and Formula for Wealth may also give you confidence and help motivate you to do what you know that you should do.

I was not born into abject poverty, but my family certainly was not well off. As a teenager I worked minimum wage jobs and after high school, I went to a vocational school so that I could move up to a better job. I continued working while I went to junior college and also after I transferred to a university. After graduating college with an engineering degree and a small amount of student debt, I got a good job, paid off my debt and started saving some money. It would have been nice to have started saving earlier. Since I worked my way through college, I was older than most when I graduated and could start saving, but I started when I could. I saved up for a down payment on a house and bought a house a couple of years after college. While working full time, I attended graduate school part-time and earned a master's degree in business. You do not need a graduate degree or even a college degree to improve your finances.

I have taken many classes in finance and learned about calls, puts, short selling and many other things you don't use in normal life. I have strived to make this book practical, easy to understand, and useful. I have been investing for a few decades and have done well following the Formula for Wealth. I have done well enough to retire comfortably and to be able pursue my hobbies.

Making everyone billionaires is beyond the abilities of this book. Helping you to be satisfied with the amount of wealth you can obtain is also beyond the abilities of this book. It will not tell you if you can do what it takes or if it is worth what it will take to build the wealth you want; those things you have to determine for yourself.

What this book is able to tell you is how much wealth you could obtain given your circumstances. The Formula for Wealth will show you how wealth grows, but how much and how fast depends on your constraints. If what you want is as much wealth as possible and as fast as possible, then the Equation for Wealth can tell you what is possible, given your constraints.

You will not need a degree in finance to use the Equation for Wealth or to apply the Formula for Wealth to your life. Just turn the page and start reading – unless you have not bought this book yet. In that case, what are you waiting for? Go buy this book!

Chapter 1

So, What is Monetary Wealth?

Before we get into the Equation for Wealth or Formula for Wealth, we have to look at what wealth is and define the factors that go into calculating wealth.

We may be able to agree that we want to be wealthier, but can we agree on what it means to be wealthy? If we are going to develop a Formula for Wealth, we will have to start with a definition of wealth. We could define wealth as good friends and good health, and we could even argue that this is the best definition of wealth. There is some truth to this, but you cannot put a monetary value on friends and family or good health, therefore, how do we fit them into a mathematical Equation for Wealth?

Fictional Friends

I would like to introduce you to a group of fictional high school friends. We will look at their lives and experiences throughout this book to help underscore the points I'm making. Any similarities between these friends and any real people are purely coincidental. Similarities should be expected since many of us have the same problems and similar difficulties.

Bobby and Erin had been dating all through high school and got tired of school and wanted nothing to do with college. Instead, Bobby and Erin got married right after they both graduated. Alex loved gadgets which helped to make the decision to study engineering in college. Blair came from a middle-class family and wanted to work in the medical field and so went to nursing school right after high school. Kyle went to a party college where he majored in girls and getting drunk. Keith was an angry kid and always in trouble. He was not planning anything after high school except to get drunk if he actually graduated. None of the friends really liked Keith except Kyle. Keith and Kyle were drinking buddies and knew where their identifications would not be checked so they could keep getting drunk. Rowan's parents were rich, which helped Rowan to get into a good college but did not help Rowan to figure out what to study.

Bobby and Erin were young and in love, so those should have been the best years of their lives. They had good friends and each other, so they should have felt rich. Were they fat, dumb and happy? While Bobby had gained some weight since they got married, they were not dumb, but it seemed that they had made some mistakes, or maybe they just did not make the right choices. Unfortunately, their bank account showed that they were having trouble paying their bills and that made them unhappy.

They were not even done thanking people for the wedding presents before they started fighting over money. They argued about spending and credit card debt, and they worried their marriage would not be able to take the strain of their financial situation. They both had jobs and worked hard, so they thought that they would get by, but they were not sure how. Could the solution to their problem be as straight forward as an equation?

Could their relationship handle the stress of their financial problems or would their marriage end in divorce, like so many others? We will come back to the story of these high school friends to see how they handle their financial problems.

Wealth can be quite relative. The Equation for Wealth deals with numbers, but not how you view these numbers. Our perceptions of any given number can change, even while the number itself does not change.

Anyone that looks at the economies of the past would have to see that the vast majority of humanity has been lifted up out of extreme poverty over the last couple of centuries. As individuals we rarely look at economics from that perspective, instead, we tend to see our finances relative to other people. What most people notice is not their actual wealth but their wealth compared to those that they know. When you have friends that are rich, then you feel poorer. When you have friends that are poor, then you feel richer.

You would think that we could all agree that professional athletes making millions should be considered wealthy. But the athletes might not agree that they are wealthy enough since they always seem to want a contract that is larger than all of the other players. If wealth is a contest, then you cannot win because there is always someone richer. Your wealth, like your health, should not really be a competition. Someone else being sick does not make you healthier, and someone else being poor does not make you wealthier.

When accumulating wealth, there gets to be a point where you will not spend the wealth that you have accumulated. What is your second million really worth to you? What is your second billion really worth to you? Does it only become a score card, or is it about power? Most of us never get to the point of having more money than we can spend, but you may want to ask yourself these questions so that you know your own motivation.

The more money you have, the less the next dollar is worth to you. So, the question is often, what is the second $100,000 or even $100 worth to you? Does it mean that you can pay your bills, feed your family or send a child to school? Is it worth what you have to give up or what you have to do for the extra money?

Once you determine what being wealthy means for you, the Equation for Wealth can tell you what it will take to get you there. Then you can determine if it is worth doing what it would take to get the wealth you are looking for. Another way to use the equation is to determine what you are willing to do, and then the Equation for Wealth can determine how wealthy you could become.

Assets, Liabilities and Net Worth

One definition of wealth might be how much stuff you have managed to acquire. By this definition you could borrow a fortune to buy stuff but be unable to pay your debt and end up bankrupt. A better definition is that wealth is the difference between what you have and what you owe. What you have minus what you owe is referred to as, using fancy economic terms, assets minus liabilities. This is your net worth. Since we are worth more than our wealth, I have wondered why it is not called net wealth.

An asset is money or anything that can be exchanged for money. Examples are savings accounts, money market accounts, certificates of deposit, stocks, bonds, real estate, etcetera. A liability is any payment that you are liable for, i.e. anything that you owe to anyone or any organization. Examples of liabilities are mortgages, leases, credit card bills, utility bills, rent bills and other bills. Buying a car that you cannot afford will cause you to take out a loan, and it is the loan that is the liability. The car that you bought with the loan would be an asset, but it could be outweighed by the liability of the loan that you had to take out. It may look like liabilities are the same as expenses, but income and expenses are not quite the same as assets and liabilities. Expenses and spending can turn into liabilities when they are not paid for right away. Income can be turned into assets when it is not spent right away on other things.

How to Calculate Net Worth and Why

You should calculate your net worth periodically in order to follow what is happening to your wealth. If you do not calculate your net worth periodically, you will not know what it was to start with or how it is changing. I used to calculate my net worth every quarter, but I have settled on figuring out my net worth yearly. How often you want to figure out your net worth is up to you. You should calculate your net worth often enough to be aware of trends, but not so much that you are watching small swings and wasting time.

You can figure out your net worth by adding up the assets (such as savings, stocks, bonds, etcetera) that you have and subtracting your liabilities (such as credit card bills, loans, etcetera); just add up what you have and subtract what you owe. Your present net worth is your current assets minus your current liabilities. So, are your liabilities (what you owe) current if they don't actually turn out to be paid later? Yes, you can only use the value of what you have (assets) and owe (liabilities) now. There is a risk that what you expect ends up failing to come true, so that changes your future net worth. A company that you invested in can go bankrupt tomorrow. Then that would change tomorrow's net worth.

I am reluctant to include pensions in net worth. The promise of a pension is really only as good as the company making the promise. Pensions can be included in net worth with the understanding that there are risks, but there are also risks to investments like stocks and bonds. To determine the worth of a pension accurately you should use the cost of an annuity that would provide the same income. You would need to get the cost of such an annuity from an agent and this may not be worth your time listening to the sales pitch that they would give you. To get an approximate value of a pension you can divide the yearly pension (what you would receive each year) by 0.04. A pension of $40,000 a year would be worth one million dollars. This would only be a ballpark number, but it is an easy way to calculate your pension's approximate worth. These days most people do not have pensions. If you do not have a pension, hopefully you have a retirement account. It's easy to know the value of a retirement account. It is whatever is in the account. What is difficult is knowing what income the retirement account will be able to provide you over a long period of time (or until you die). You can multiply the amount that is in your retirement account by 0.04 to get a general idea of the yearly income that it could provide.

When calculating your net worth, you need to be

sure to only include your current assets and liabilities. If you include what you expect your assets or liabilities will be, then you are projecting what your future net worth would be. You may expect to earn a benefit or you may have earned a benefit and expect to receive that benefit. You may expect to receive a pension when you have worked long enough, or you may have earned a pension that you expect to receive when you retire. There is a risk that you will not get what you expect, and that would affect your future net worth. When figuring out your net worth, you could include the bills that you expect to get tomorrow and you could include the payment that you expect to receive tomorrow, but then you would be projecting what your net worth could be tomorrow instead of calculating your current net worth. Do not confuse your current net worth with how much you project that your net worth could become. (We will get to projecting your future net worth in chapter 5 "The Mathematical Equation for Wealth".) You could also include your furniture, clothes, etcetera in your assets, but there really is no reason to try to be that accurate.

For your liabilities you should use what it would currently take to pay off your debts. The important thing is to choose what you want to include in your asset and liability lists and be consistent with those lists each time you perform your calculation.

You could attempt to place a monetary value on skills, knowledge, abilities and other less direct measures of wealth but this may prove to be difficult, inaccurate and not worth the effort. How do we account for the value of an education and a career? You could try to figure out the present value of your future earnings and you will get a good idea of what your education and career should be worth, but who wants to go through that much math? And you don't have too. The value of your career is indirectly included in your net worth by the assets that you purchase from your income during your career. Not everything needs to be or can be included in your net worth. Be consistent in what you include so that you can see the trends in your net worth.

Obsessing over exactly how much net worth you have may not help you to be satisfied with your accuracy or the amount of your wealth. Having accountants to keep track of all that you have and how much you owe may not be enough for you to be satisfied. You could get to the point where it is not possible for you to figure out what you have because it is growing faster than you can count it, and yet it may still not be enough for you to be satisfied. It is up to you to determine what is enough to be content and how accurate you need to be to know how much you have (your current net worth).

You get to choose how much detail you use to calculate net worth and how much effort you put into figuring out something that is changing. I prefer to put the effort into figuring out how it is changing so that I can figure out how to change my net worth the way that I want. Tracking your net worth is similar to tracking your weight on a scale while dieting. As long as you continue to use the same scale, you can keep track of your progress, even if that scale is off a little. Whatever way you calculate your net worth, please be consistent so you can see how your net worth is changing. When you change how you calculate your net worth, the change in net worth from changing how you calculate will make it hard to see other changes to your net worth.

As an example of calculating net worth: If you have a house that is worth $500,000 and you owe $300,000 on that house, then the net worth of your home is $200,000: $500,000 asset minus $300,000 liability equals a net worth of $200,000. If you also have a car that is worth $20,000 (asset), but you owe $15,000 (liability), then adding it to the net worth of your home, your net worth is $205,000. When you add assets of a savings account of $5,000 and a retirement account of $20,000, you would get a total net worth of $230,000. But if you also have credit card debt of $10,000 (liability), then your net worth is $220,000.

Let's look at an example of why calculating net worth is important. Bobby and Erin worked hard but never seemed to get anywhere. Their parents also worked hard but were never able to retire because they never seemed to get ahead of their bills. Bobby and Erin are worried if the same thing would happen to them. Like many of us there were storms in their lives, and they often struggled against strong headwinds just to make ends meet. Bobby and Erin spent a lot of their time arguing about money. They both worked to earn money, and they both spent money, but they did not work together to control their spending. Instead, they both just spent what they wanted to and then argued about not having enough money. One year they were expecting to get a bonus from work, so they both spent the bonus, even before they got the bonus. That year the company had had a bad year and did not give out any bonuses. They had spent twice the amount of the expected bonus only to receive nothing. That ended up increasing their credit card debt even more. Out of frustration they yelled a lot and blamed each other for their problems.

Bobby had heard about being able to calculate a household's net worth and wanted to calculate how much they had, so Bobby gave it a try. Bobby and Erin were leasing their car and renting an apartment. Their credit card debt was greater than what little savings they had, so when they calculated their net worth, they found out that it was negative. They owed more than what they owned. It was the wakeup call that they needed. Bobby and Erin finally talked to each other about their problem and vowed to find a better solution than fighting.

Changes to Net Worth

What changes net worth? Only things that change your assets or liabilities can change your net worth. Your wealth is what you have minus what you owe.

To increase your wealth, you can either have more or owe less. When you consume more than you create, your wealth will decrease. When you create more than you consume, then your wealth will increase. That sure sounds simple. In the big picture it really is that simple. We can make it sound more complicated, of course. And someone who is really trying to make it more complicated may be trying to sell you something. If you never do more than increase assets and reduce liabilities, you will still have a good understanding of how to grow your wealth. Of course, I recommend, for the best results, that you read this entire book and do a bit more than that.

Income and Expenses

Income and wealth are not the same. It is not your income that matters for building wealth, it is the assets that you acquire with your income. This means that you cannot spend all of your income and still buy assets such as stocks and bonds to build your wealth. Spending a lot does not mean that you have a lot; it means that you are consuming a lot of what you have. Even when you earn a small fortune, you will end up broke if you are spending a large fortune. We have all heard of the celebrity or athlete that spent all of their income and ended up being broke. When you spend your time and money partying, you cannot expect to still have money when you decide it is time to invest for the future. We have also all heard of the janitor that ends up being a millionaire because he saved his money and made the right investments. Having a large income does give you more opportunities to build wealth, but you still need to make use of the opportunities that you have. You can make the best use of the opportunities that you have whether they are great or small. You can also develop new opportunities and ways to increase your income.

Income is not the same as an asset and an expense is not the same as liability. Income leads to assets when the income is used to buy assets. You could also create an asset, such as building a house. By writing this book, I believe that I have created an asset. Expenses lead to liabilities when the expenses are not paid off. Even though they are not the same, you can see that there is a strong relationship between income and assets and between expenses and liabilities.

Decrease Your Liabilities

Financial liabilities and debts are really the same thing. One of the latest trends in borrowing is online installment loans. No matter what you call debt, it is still borrowing. Whatever you call your debt, it is still just a way to refer to what you owe.

Changing the value of our liabilities is done by paying off debt, changing the interest on the existing debt or taking on new debt. One person's liability is typically another person's asset. For example, the loan you took from your bank is your liability and the bank's asset. Do you really want your debt to increase someone else's wealth? Since liabilities are subtracted from assets, you want the lowest interest rate on your liabilities that you can get. The best interest rate on debt is zero, which is only obtained when you have no debt.

Reducing liabilities is straight forward but not necessarily easy. You reduce liabilities by not borrowing and by paying back what you have borrowed. When the growth of your liabilities is greater than the growth of your assets, you are getting poorer. The way to reduce liabilities is to pay off your debt. You do that by spending less or earning more. Even better is to both spend less and earn more, which will allow you to pay off your debt even faster.

Conventional wisdom says that you should pay off the debt that has the highest interest rate first. Paying off debts with the highest interest makes mathematical sense. Paying off debts that have the smallest balance allows you to succeed at your goal and is encouraging, so it makes emotional sense. Paying off debt with the highest interest rate first or the lowest balance first will work to pay off debt. You will pay a little less if you choose to pay off debt with the highest interest rate first. What really matters is that you have a plan to pay off your debt, that you keep to your plan and pay off your debt. What really matters is that you keep spending less that you earn and you keep using the difference to pay off your debt. Paying off debts and keeping at it makes economic sense. Even when debt does not cause bankruptcy it still costs you the money that you pay in interest, money that is no longer available to be used elsewhere.

Focus is often placed on debt because at any given moment it is what we can work on. Not all debt is bad; it depends on whether what you get is worth the cost. Going into debt for a house is normally a good idea and about the only way that you can manage to buy a house. Buying a house that you cannot afford or buying *anything* that you cannot afford is not a good idea. Debt from school may pay off in the future, but then again, it may not. Use debt sparingly and wisely.

Increase Your Assets

Increasing the value of the assets you have or adding more assets to the assets you already have is how you increase your assets. Selling your assets doesn't decrease your assets; it really just changes it from one type of asset to another, namely from what you had to the cash that you got from the sale. When you have a change in the value of an asset, it is called the return on your investment. There will be more on this later, but for now we will move on to getting more assets.

If you buy something that you can afford, then the value of that asset can increase your wealth. If you buy something that has very little value, then your wealth increases very little. And if you buy something with a great deal of value, then your wealth increases greatly. Remember, the cash you are spending is also an asset, so the change in your wealth is the difference between the cash you spend and the value of the asset that you buy. When you exchange cash to buy another asset, what matters is if you get a good deal so that you are not overpaying for the asset and how the value of the asset changes after you have bought it.

How you get more assets starts with getting more income than you are spending. Which means you either have to increase your income or decrease your spending. The normal way to acquire assets is from your income, and the most common income is wages. You can also be given assets such as an inheritance, or you could win an asset such as the lottery. Wages may be the most common way to increase the value of your assets, but it is not the only way. Income can also be from rental property, stock dividends, royalties, interest from bonds, etcetera. One popular way to increase the value of your assets is to buy a fixer-up house, then the labor and materials that you put into fixing up the house increases the value of that asset. The increased value you put into the house is how you can profit by fixing up the house and flipping it. But for most of us our income is the wages from our jobs.

Chapter 2

Personal Finance:
The First Step to Wealth

Budgeting

The most obvious way to have money is to not spend it. Of course, that is easier said than done. What you should be able to do is to spend less than you earn and therefore have some money left over. If you can control your spending and keep spending to less than your income without a budget, then that would be fine, you will be increasing your wealth. But you would be one of the few that can control spending without knowing what you are spending. Most of us have trouble keeping control of our spending, even when we know what our spending is and we know that we are losing control of our spending. You should not expend a lot of effort or money keeping track of your spending; you should not spend dollars keeping track of dimes. You should not even spend dimes keeping track of dollars. You should be able to spend just a little time and keep your own records, unless you have millions and need to hire accountants.

Credit cards are one of the most common spending problems. It can be very easy to spend using credit cards without really knowing how much you are spending. Credit cards can separate your thoughts of what you are spending from how much you are *really* spending. Using credit cards may not seem as real as spending cash, so it can be hard to realize how much you are spending. If credit cards are making it hard for you to budget and control your spending, then you should think of getting rid of your credit cards. When your credit card spending is out of control and you are having trouble paying off your credit cards, then it is definitely time to stop using your credit cards and to get rid of them.

Toward the end of the month do you find that there is more month left than money? Without some form of a budget you have no idea what you are spending your money on. At the end of the month you could end up broke and have no idea where the money went. A budget does not change the amount of money you have or the amount of your expenses but a budget gives you knowledge of what you spend, so that you can have some control and you have a chance to have more money left over at the end of the month.

To spend less than you make, you will need to know how much you spend. To know how much you spend, you will need a budget. A budget is really just a record of how much you spend each month. What you do with this information is up to you. A budget helps you to know how much you are spending and what you are spending it on. A budget does not help you to have the will and discipline to control your spending. You will still need the self-control to follow through with your decision of how you will spend what you earn. A budget helps you to understand where your money is going, and it is up to you to choose how you will spend your money.

Failing to plan is planning to fail, whether you call it a plan or a budget. So, develop a budget, evaluate how your plan/budget is doing and adjust accordingly. Establish your budget and then modify it when your life and desires change.

How detailed should the plan/budget be? It is your plan so you decide. The important thing is to have a plan. A bad plan is better than no plan. A bad plan is at least a starting point for making adjustments and improvements. There is no reason to keep a bad plan. Keep changing your plan until you get it right. Do not expect your plan to be perfect; you should expect to always be improving your plan. If nothing else, your desires will change and that will change your plan. Your plan, or your budget, is nothing more than what you want and how you think that you can get what you want.

My first budget was very basic but allowed me to make sure I was able to pay my rent, utilities and food. It was detailed enough for a starting point. When I got married, my wife expanded on it and made a ledger for our budget. Making a budget that is too complicated can cause frustration, which could cause you to give up on the budget. Try to create a budget that keeps track of your spending but is also simple enough that you continue to follow your budget. You need to have a plan while also being flexible so you can alter your plan as things change.

A budget is your plan for the future; it is what you are planning to spend. When you are successful at living within your budget, then the budget becomes a record of what you did spend. It is up to you to make the plan and execute the plan. When making a budget, be careful to separate your wants from what your real needs are, account for all of your expenses and be realistic.

The basic way to make a budget is to add up what you absolutely have to spend (such as rent, utilities and food) and subtract this from your net income, which, hopefully, will give you your discretionary income. Discretionary income is your non-essential spending. If this is negative (i.e., your income is less than your essential expenses), then you have a real problem. You would have to start working on increasing your income and decreasing your rent, utilities and food. Your discretionary income is what you can use to pay off your debt, save, invest and spend a little of it on things you enjoy. When making a budget, there are three ways to go about it. 1) You can start with the income that you have and try to fit your expenses into it. 2) You can start with your expenses and see what income you have left. Or 3) you can also do a combination of the two until you can spend less that you earn and have some left to pay off debt and start saving.

One budget plan to use as a starting point is as follows: use half of your take-home pay for essentials, 30 percent of your take home pay for general spending and then 20 percent of your take home pay for long-term financial goals. Long-term financial goals would be such things as paying off debt, investing in retirement accounts or saving to replace your car. If you use this plan, you would then see if half of your take-home pay would cover your mortgage (or rent), utilities, food, transportation, insurance and property tax (your essentials). If half of your after-tax income did not cover your essentials, then you would have to reduce how much was available for general spending and your long-term financial goals. You would then continue to make adjustments until you determined how you wanted to spend your income.

There are plenty of budget plans available out there. Using one of them as a starting point may save you the work of coming up with something on your own. Whatever plan you start with, make it your own by changing it to suit your life. A budget may say that you should have 25 percent of your income for housing, but you live in New York City and cannot find any housing for less than 35 percent of your income. So, you have to adjust the budget. Get a starting point for your budget and adjust it as you need to.

Budgetary Goals

When developing a budget, you will need to determine what you really want. Do you want to spend now or pay off debt, or save and invest for a house, retirement or other future desires? So in your budget you need to set aside an amount for saving and investing because if you wait until the end of the month to figure out what you have left to save, there will not be anything left, and you will never start saving and investing. You might have a good plan to get rid of your debt and then start saving and investing, but what matters is what you do. If you plan to reduce your debt but you keep on spending more than you earn, then you will only be increasing your debt.

Of course, you want to keep your spending low. If your budget is too tight for you to stay with that budget, then you may have trouble continuing to spend less than you earn. In order to keep to your budget, it may help to think about more than just the numbers; remember what you wanted to do with your savings and investments.

Cash Flow Crisis

You never know what problems the future will bring so you need to have some readily available money to take care of the unexpected problems that come up. You save for the unexpected by doing two things: spend less than you earn, and do not spend what you plan to earn until you have it. You may be expecting to get a certain amount of money each month, but things happen that you can't predict. Planning for the future is wise, but you also have to plan for the unexpected. Acting as if you already have what you are planning on can lead to problems when those plans fall through or something happens that you weren't expecting.

There are some who figure out how much they can afford to spend by the size of the payments that they can make. Realize that this does not build wealth except for those that you are borrowing from. If you have assets of half a million dollars and you have debts of half a million dollars, they cancel out and you are left with no net worth. If all of your income is going to making payments, then you are only one problem away from a crisis.

Financial crises, whether personal or national, tend to come from excessive borrowing, lack of diversification and/or the mismatch between liabilities and assets. The mismatch between assets and liabilities could be from assets that are difficult to sell, such as having real estate and short-term liabilities such as monthly bills. This is sometimes called being house rich and cash poor. When the debt is due, you may not have the money to pay the bill. This might force you to sell quickly at a loss to avoid facing foreclosure. Although you have the assets (such as real estate or a retirement account) to cover your liabilities, you may have difficulty converting the assets into cash quickly or without significant tax penalties in order to pay your debt.

A fancy term for readily available money is liquid assets. This could be cash, silver, gold, savings, money market, etcetera. If any financial advisor does not advise having some readily available money, then you should really question their advice. You can expect to get a wide range of advice from financial advisors because there is not a set amount that is right for everyone. Since we have different levels of risk that we tolerate, there are different levels of readily available money that are advisable. (There will be more on risk tolerance later.) Some would say that you need enough readily available money to cover 3 months, 6 months or even a year of expenses. Some may advise that you have a set amount of money (such as $25,000 or $50,000) readily available. I would say that you need some money available and how much depends on how much you are willing to risk not being able to deal with problems as they arise. You need enough funds to stop a problem from becoming a crisis. You should also take into account how likely you are to have a problem. If you have a steady job, you would be less likely to have a large problem than if your job is seasonal or subject to frequent layoffs. You need to have money readily available, but how much will depend on your individual situation and how much risk you are comfortable with.

So then why not put all of your money in these liquid assets? The reason to limit how much is in liquid assets is that you do not normally make as much on them as you could with other investments. The most liquid asset is cash, but you will not earn any interest on the money that you carry around in your wallet. Your checking account is a liquid asset, but you would make more interest from a certificate of deposit (CD) than from money in your checking account. Gold and silver are liquid assets, but most of the time you will make more money from stocks. Having liquid assets costs you what you could have made from other investment opportunities. A fancy term for this is opportunity cost.

Having some readily available money set aside in order to avoid a cash flow crisis is part of investing wisely because it can help you avoid being forced to sell at a loss. When you need money, you may be desperate and not thinking rationally. You may be tempted to get a high interest loan or sell something for far less than it is worth. Desperation can make you do things that you don't really want to do. Thinking ahead by budgeting, sticking to the budget and having some liquid assets may help you to avoid getting into desperate situations.

Bobby and Erin

Do you remember how the fictional couple Bobby and Erin had no control over their spending? Neither Bobby nor Erin wanted to be so far in debt. They each knew a budget would be helpful, but still did not work

as a team and therefore they each made their own bud-
gets. That did not work out well for them. It needed to
be *their* budget. Just as it would only take one of them
to blow their budget and assure failure, it would take
both of them working together to make their budget
work. They both needed to agree to the budget, and
then they both needed to commit to the budget.

After some arguing, they finally sat down and
made a budget they could both live with. When they
paid their essential expenses, they discovered they
could save a little bit by making a few changes. Bobby
stopped going to the bar every night for a beer after
work, and Erin stopped drinking overpriced coffee
every morning. They both cut back everywhere they
could and only allowed themselves a couple of small
indulgences.

To speed up the process of getting out of debt,
Bobby and Erin both got second jobs, which increased
their income. They got jobs that were flexible and
allowed them to schedule the new hours around their
existing work schedule. They ended up working so
much at first that they didn't see much of each other
anymore. They decided to set aside a regular night for
themselves and rearranged their budget so they could
have consistent date nights.

After they paid off their credit card debt, Bobby
and Erin were able to save up enough money to buy
a car without going into debt. They were able to get
a good deal on a slightly used car, and they bought it
with cash. Over time, they also were able to save up for

a down payment on a house, so they could stop paying rent. They bought a duplex that they could afford. It needed some work, but they got a good deal, and they rented out half of it to help pay the mortgage. They may not have been handy with tools, but with the help of family, friends and the hardware store staff they figured out how to do the work that was needed on the duplex. So, they owned a car and a house, and only owed on their mortgage. Now when they calculated their net worth, it was positive because they owned more than they owed. Before long, Bobby and Erin had a child, so they needed to rearrange their budget again for their new expenses. As life happens, their budget could be rearranged for the changes in their lives.

Bobby and Erin did not set aside anything for emergencies in the first budget that they made. When their washing machine broke down, they ended up going back into debt to get it replaced. The next budget that they made did include setting aside some money for those unexpected things that come up.

Chapter 3

Wealth Management: The Second Step to Wealth

Return on Investment

The Formula for Wealth is to spend less than you earn and invest the difference wisely for as long as you can. We have already covered the first step in chapter 2 "Personal Finance: The First Step to Wealth." The way to acquire assets and increase your wealth is to make more than you spend. Spending less than you earn comes down to either earning more and/or spending less. But just making more than you spend is not enough to ensure wealth if the assets you acquire with your income lose their value. The next factor in the Formula for Wealth that you can control, is to invest wisely. So that is the next step to wealth.

When you can find things that are more valuable than their cost, then when you invest in them, you will make a financial gain. You could shop at garage sales and find an antique that is worth more than what you have to pay for it. In which case your wealth would increase, but you are not likely to get rich at garage sales. You cannot normally find things that cost less than they are worth. Normally, you pay what it is worth at the time that you invest in it and then the value changes with time. You could pay fair market price for some real estate, and then next year a large company wants to build in the area, so the value of the real estate goes up and your wealth increases.

When assets become more valuable over time than what their initial cost was, then this is what is called return on investment (ROI). Rate of return (ROR), return on equity (ROE), return on investment and interest rate are all very similar ways to measure the growth (or loss) of your assets. They all tell you how much your investments are changing over time. I want to avoid the complications from separating stocks, bonds, real estate, companies and debt, so I'll lump them all together as return on investment (ROI).

Return on investment needs to account for all returns minus all costs of the investment as well as the total of all of the investments. This can add a lot to the complexity, which could be simplified by averaging the returns on your investments or using the average return from groups of investments. The return on investment also has to be in the same time frame that you are using in the equation. When you are using yearly return on investment, then your time frame that you use in the equation must also be yearly.

The question you want to ask yourself when looking at investing is What will be worth the most next year relative to its cost? The better you are able to forecast this, the higher your rate of return will be at the end of the year. Forecasting what the rate of return will be on your investment can be less than straight forward. You need to prevent your desires from coloring your view of reality. You may really have enjoyed your vacation, but that does not mean that the time-share you stayed in would turn out to be a good investment.

Relationship of Return on Investment and Financial Risk

There is always risk with any investment; there is no investment that is sure to be a good investment. If there was a sure thing, then everyone would invest in it and the price would go up until it was no longer such a good investment.

Some may say that it is best to get the highest rate of return possible on your investments and the lowest risk possible. Unfortunately, you will not be able to get both the highest rate of return and the lowest risk on your investment. Normally high rates of return on investments are associated with high risk investments and low risk investments are associated with low rates of return on investments. Many venture capitalists seek out risk because they want the higher return. They do not really want the higher risk, but they know that is where they will find higher returns. If you take a greater risk and buy an investment that you hope will make 12 percent return on your investment and then end up losing your investment because it did not perform as well as you hoped, you will be far worse off than if you were able to get 8 percent on a lower-risk investment. If you believe that getting the highest return possible is what matters to you, then you are saying that risk does not matter and any level of risk is acceptable to you. What really matters is the risk that is acceptable to you. What is best for you is the highest rate of return that you can get on your investment at the level of risk that is acceptable to you. This is called risk tolerance.

Risk Tolerance

You may be the daredevil type who would jump out of a plane for the thrill of it. You may be the type that would climb a mountain because it is there. You could be the type that does not take chances, who has a security system that includes a safe room, security cameras everywhere and extra locks on your windows and doors. The same concept applies to investing. Some people like to take chances when investing and some do not. If you are worrying about your investments and staying up nights thinking about your investments, then you are taking too many chances with your investments. If your worry is that you will not have enough invested, then maybe you will need to take more chances and invest more. Not all risk is in the items that you invest in. You can also take risk in how *much* you invest. By spending less, looking for a better paying job or getting an education for a better paying career, you are taking risks so that you can have more to invest.

How much do the ups and downs of your investments bother your piece of mind, and how much is your piece of mind worth to you? This would be another way of saying what your risk tolerance is. How much risk is right for you? Is it worth the probability of going broke for a chance at getting rich? What can you be satisfied with? What level of risk do you feel comfortable with? These are the type of questions you should ask yourself, so you know what types of investments are right for you. When a financial advisor does not want to know what level of risk is acceptable to you, then they are trying to sell you their investment product instead of the investment that is right for you.

It can be good to avoid risks. Taking risks can get you killed or injured. You would not risk going to a more dangerous country for a new job that pays what you are making now. The amount of raise it would take to get you to go to a dangerous country is a sign of what your risk tolerance is.

Most people would rather miss the chance of gaining money than risk losing money. When there is no risk, there is also no gain. When investing, you cannot completely avoid risk. Trying too hard to avoid risk will also mean missing opportunities to make money. Over time and over many risk-taking investors, the odds generally favor risk takers, but the individual investor could also lose a lot. You need to determine how much risk is right for you.

When you are a couple like Bobby and Erin, you need to take into account the risk tolerance for each of you. Bobby liked to play it safe and Erin liked to take chances and push the envelope trying to get higher returns on their investments. So, they had to work together and come up with a compromise as to how risky their investments would be. They compromised and had a risky portfolio that was just not quite as risky as Erin wanted.

Financial crashes are not always predictable. If they were, then investors would have already moved their money out of those investments before the crash. There are some things that can be done to prepare for investment risks, but there are always risks. When you feel comfortable with your investment because you think that you are prepared enough for the unexpected then you have reached your risk tolerance. This is another way to illustrate your risk tolerance.

Good luck finding any risk-free investment, except perhaps paying off your own debt. Relatively safe types of investments would be cash, gold, silver, saving accounts, certificate of deposit, and bonds. Bonds are considered safe, but there is the risk that inflation will be higher than the rate of return on the bonds, in which case your real return is negative because the return on your investment does not keep up with the increased prices that you are paying. Riskier types of investments would be stocks, mutual funds and exchange-traded funds. And if you really want risk, you can invest in penny stocks and junk bonds.

Risk in assets and financial markets cannot be precisely calculated because you do not really know the odds of what will happen. Investment returns are uncertain and variable, as asset values can go up and down. There may be a probable rate of return, but almost anything can happen. (This is a good reason for diversification, but that is another subject that we will get to soon.) We end up needing to rely on estimates and educated guesses, so you need to choose the general level of risk that is acceptable to you.

The expected rate of return is the average of all the likely rates of return. If you bet on the flip of a coin and half the time you gain a dollar and the other half of the time you lose a dollar, then they cancel out and there is no expected change from placing the bet. If this bet was an investment, then there would be no expected rate of return on your investment. What happens if there is a revolution in a country that you invested in? You would expect to get a negative return on your investments, and you may be glad if you can get back any of your investment. Of course, if you expect this outcome, then you would not have invested in that country in the first place. If a revolution is possible, then there would have to be the chance for very good profits in order to increase the expected rate of return and get you to take a chance and invest in that country.

If you play the lottery, you may strike it rich, but most of the time you will lose what you invested. The expected return would be negative. If you expect to lose your money, why would anyone play the lottery? Most people only spend a couple of dollars on the lottery, so it has little impact on them. If you spend ten dollars out of $1000 on the lottery and invest the other portion at an expected return of 10 percent, then your total expected return would be ninety-nine dollars [($1000 - $10) x 0.1 = $990 x 0.1 = $99], which would be 9.9 percent total expected return. People play the lottery because they are willing to accept the expected return for the overall risk. Playing the lottery could be very risky, but if most of your money is in a safe investment, your overall risk (your risk with your investments combined with your risk playing the lottery) is lower, and it is easier to accept a lower expected return for a chance at hitting it big.

If your dream is to make a fortune as a professional athlete or to hit it big as an actor or actress, then you had better not quit your day job. Maybe your odds are not as bad as hitting the lottery, but the odds are very much against you. If you do want really high risk, then put aside enough to pay for your food and housing. When you put your money in a very risky investment, then you will most likely lose your money. Trying to hit a home run and swinging for the fences gives you a better chance of striking out. Persistent base hits add up, so it may be better to get a base hit and not strike out. You don't know how many chances you will have to get up to bat in life. It is your life and it is your choice, but your choice should be an informed choice made based on your tolerance of risk.

If you have a very secure career, you could take greater risks with your investments. When you have an insecure career, you need to be safer with your investments, so that you can protect yourself against downturns in your career, such as when you have a job that may result in layoffs when there is a recession. Then you need a larger amount of safe assets to be able to ride out the layoffs. If your career is in a boom and bust industry, then you need to use some of the money that you make during the boom times to help pay your bills during the busts. In a way this is self-insurance for what could be expected in an insecure career, such as construction.

There are those that calculate risk-adjusted returns to measure if they are investing well. I am not convinced that it is appropriate for individuals, and I do not think that it is worth the effort for the average person. It is far easier to determine the level of risk that you are comfortable with and then strive for the highest rate of return at that level of risk.

The idea of mixing risky and safe investments is quite common. The goal is to get a better return on your investments at an acceptable level of risk. Investors will often do this by putting some money in risky stocks in hopes of higher returns and some of their money in safer blue chips stocks or bonds. One common way is to mix 60 percent stocks with 40 percent bonds. There are numerous options on what is the best mix to maximize the rate of return while keeping the risk manageable.

One issue with coming up with the best mix is that we all have different levels of risk that we find acceptable. The level of risk that we find acceptable also changes. Normally, we accept more risk when we are young and less as we get older. World affairs can also change how much risk we are willing to take. When the outside environment is safe, we are normally riskier with our investments. Many times, a drop in the stock market has been caused by world affairs such as conflicts. Investors are scared by rumors of war, so they sell riskier assets, and the price of those riskier assets fall while they buy safer assets, and the price of those safer assets rise. After a catastrophe you may become more reluctant to take risks. Changes to your risk tolerance are normal, but they may be an overreaction to an event. Unless there are going to be more wars or more disasters than before, previous disasters should not change the investment risks that you take today. You should base your current investments on what you think will happen in the future.

A wise investment for someone else may not be the right investment for you. Wise investments for you depend on your goals and what risk you are comfortable with. You can use the Equation for Wealth to see what rate of return you would need to reach your goals. This will help you decide what level of risk is needed to meet your goals. If you are uncomfortable with the level of risk associated with the needed rate of return, then you may need to adjust your goal.

No matter what investment option you choose, diversification of your investments is a wise choice.

Diversification

Entire books are written arguing about what it is to invest wisely. What it means to invest wisely can be debatable, but there are some things that we should be able to agree on. If your employer offers matching contributions to a retirement account, then it is wise to get all of the matching funds that you can. If you have debt, then it is wise to pay off your debt. When it comes to investing, it is wise to diversify your investments. How to best diversify can be argued and depends on the risk that you are willing to take. But no one is going to tell you not to diversify your investments unless perhaps they are trying to sell you their investment product.

Diversification allows you to reduce the chance that one bad investment costs you everything. The old adage 'don't put all of your eggs in one basket' applies to diversification because if something happens to that basket, you will lose all of your eggs. Or at least you'll have to figure out how to make scrambled eggs. This same idea is true with money. Don't put all of your money into one investment or even one type of investment.

I have made mistakes, who hasn't. Being diversified

has reduced the damage done from my investment mistakes. I would be wealthier today if I had bought stocks instead of a sports car. If I had known which tech stock was going to take off, I probably would have bought that stock instead. When investing in stocks, most gains come from a handful of hot stocks. Other than hindsight how would you really know which stock will be one of the hot stocks? Enron had been considered to be a hot stock at one time, but then it went bust and you would have lost your money if you had invested in that trendy stock. What is thought to be a good investment today can turn out to be a poor investment. Diversification gives you a better chance of buying one of the stocks that really do turn out to be a hot stock. To invest wisely you do not need to always pick the next hot stock, you can pick lots of solid stocks and have one of them turn out to be the next hot stock.

I have made some mistakes but I have also gotten some things right. Sometimes I did not even have anything to do with what went right, such as being fortunate enough to be born in the United States. I was also fortunate to invest when mutual funds and index funds were available. Just like me, sometimes you may not have anything to do with what goes right or what goes badly for you. No matter how smart or wise you are, some things are out of our control. You cannot avoid mistakes, but being diversified could avoid having a mistake turn into a disaster.

Diversity would be having multiple types of investments such as cash, gold, real estate, stocks and bonds. Having both stocks and bonds helps to diversify because most of the time when the value of stocks is falling, the value of bonds are rising. For diversity you could have both domestic stock funds and foreign stock funds. Also, for diversity you could have both government bond funds and corporate bond funds. Government bonds are generally considered safe but even governments default on their debts sometimes.

Types of Investment Vehicles

With many people needing to save for retirement, the market has developed many ways to invest their savings. We are not stuck with just savings accounts and saving bonds. There has been an explosion of investment options over the last few decades. It seems that there are more mutual funds and exchange-traded funds then there are stocks that are traded.

Real Estate

Real estate can be a wise type of investment. There are two types of real estate investments: commercial and residential. Many people have made money in rental property, but for most people their greatest asset is the equity in their home.

Real estate can be a good investment if you buy in the right location or even if you just avoid paying rent. Real estate investment has been the path for many to become millionaires. Real estate can be hard to sell when you need to, especially if everyone is trying to sell real estate at the same time. You can avoid this becoming a crisis if you have enough other assets that are easier to sell.

Rental property or investment property has long been the way to grow wealth. It can still be an investment with a good return on your investment, especially if you choose the right area. Rental property can also be a lot of work and very aggravating when you get a few difficult tenants. You can hire a property manager to help with the work, but this will lower the return on your investment. Investing in rental property could also be subject to the risk of rent controls and rising property taxes.

Real estate is expensive, so investing in it for diversification can be difficult. You might look at publicly listed real estate investment trusts (REITS) as a less expensive way to invest in real estate without buying the real estate yourself. Another way would be to invest in a duplex or fourplex and live in one of the units while renting out the other units. If you get a duplex or fourplex that needs fixing up, you could fix up units while living in one of them.

Housing is a common way to accumulate wealth. Home ownership is a large portion of the wealth for middle-class families. Real estate can be a good investment, but it is not a sure thing as the area you invested in could have the major employer shut down or even worse it could become a war zone.

For most of the richest households, stocks and

bonds make up a greater portion of their wealth than real estate.

Stocks

Another common type of investment is stocks, and there are a lot of types of stocks. There are different ways to refer to the characteristics of stocks: income, growth, blue chip, small cap, mid cap, and large cap. No matter how you classify the stock, it is the condition of the company that you are buying stock in that matters. It is not wise to buy stock in an unprofitable, poorly run company, no matter how you classify the stock. If you do not understand what you are thinking about investing in, then stop considering that investment until you understand it. When you are buying stocks, learn about the company that you are investing in. It is common to use internet searches or company provided information such as a prospectus. You should be careful not to rely solely on information that comes directly or indirectly from the company that you are investing in.

Mutual Funds

If you do not enjoy researching companies, you could invest in mutual funds. To diversify using mutual funds, the mutual funds need to be different types of funds. When you have multiple funds from the same category, you are not really diversifying. In fact, the funds may be holding mostly the same stocks. To diversify you would want funds from different categories such as growth, income, international, small cap and large cap.

When you buy mutual funds, you will pay a management fee. The management of the fund is not worth one percent. If your fund charges more than a one percent annual fund expense, start looking for another fund. You could find annual fees of 0.2 percent or less. In addition, some funds are what is called loaded funds. Loaded funds charge you to buy into the fund. The fee for buying a loaded fund is really just a sales commission. Looking into no-load funds is a way to avoid paying this commission.

Index Funds

It is hard for small investors to compete with institutional investors such as pension funds that have a great deal of resources. The growth of computerized investing and artificial intelligence has made it even harder for an investor to do better than the market. It might be wise to accept the market return by using index funds, especially the lower cost index funds. An index fund is made up of a representative sample of a group of investments, such as the Dow Jones Industrial Average. Index funds can give investors access to a diversified portfolio for only a fraction of a percent in fees.

I like low-cost index funds since I am a lazy

investor that likes getting the diversity without having to pick individual stocks. It is unlikely that I could really do better than the market. Index funds and mutual funds allow the small investor like myself to be able to easily diversify. I have bought funds in sectors that I thought would do well, but I also have funds in multiple sectors. A sector can be any distinct portion of the economy, and some of them may do well while other are doing poorly. I am not recommending any particular index or fund. What I am recommending is investing in as many different stocks, indexes and/or funds as practical for as much diversity as practical.

Lately, the American economy has been doing well, and the American stock markets have done better than other rich-world markets. No stock market can outperform the other markets forever. If you are solely in American markets, then when the market goes down, it could be very costly. For Americans, not only would your portfolio drop so would the economy, causing more unemployment. The currency would also drop, causing the cost of imports to increase. To avoid being overexposed to a drop in one market, you can diversify using a global stock index, an emerging market index or a combination of indexes.

Exchange-Traded Funds

Exchange-Traded Funds (ETF) are also a good way to diversify. Exchange-traded funds are basically a mutual fund that is traded on a market, like a stock.

There are numerous exchange-traded funds available to choose from, and they are easily traded. You could treat the exchange-traded funds like stocks and trade them, trying to do better than the market. A real advantage of exchange-traded funds is that they represent a sector (or section) of the market. There is an exchange-traded fund for almost any sector; you could even buy an exchange-traded fund for the cannabis sector. When you believe that something like health care will be the next hot investment, you can buy a health care sector exchange-traded fund without having to pick an individual stock. Yesterday's hot sector or hot stock may not be tomorrow's hot sector. When a sector is in vogue, then it may already have risen in price and may not continue to do better than the rest of the market. You would need to be able to predict what sector will be the next hot sector if you are going to be able to do better than the market, just like you would need to do with stocks.

Why pay high cost brokerage commissions? When buying index funds, mutual funds or exchange-traded funds, look at all of the fund charges. Some funds have fees for starting and/or closing an account, so look for low total cost. Yes, it will cost you something, but there is quite a range in what you could be charged.

Our fictional couple, Bobby and Erin, invested some of their time into getting an education that applied to their careers. The added education resulted in getting new jobs that included raises and benefits. One of these benefits was that their employer would match a portion of their contribution to a retirement account. So, Bobby and Erin used the raises that they got from their new jobs to contribute to a retirement account and thereby got the matching contribution that the company offered. Bobby and Erin invested the funds of their retirement account in multiple, low-cost index funds. They also quit their second jobs and invested more of their time with each other and their family.

Bonds

Yet another type of wise investment is bonds. There are numerous types of bonds: municipal, treasury, savings, mortgage backed, corporate, junk bonds and bond funds. There are even subsets of these types of bonds. Generally, bonds are as safe as the entity issuing the bond, so savings bonds and treasury bonds are as safe as the government, and corporate bonds are as safe as the company that issued them. Income from savings bonds and treasury bonds are not taxed by state and local governments, and income from municipal bonds are not taxed by the federal government. These tax breaks from treasury and municipal bonds can make a difference when your tax bracket is high.

The value of existing bonds goes up when interest rates go down and generally go up when stocks are going down, such as during a recession. When you have stocks, you can use bonds to diversify. While stocks go down during a recession, interest rates also go down. This causes the value of the bonds that you have to go up. So having both stocks and bonds can be a good way to reduce the risk to your investments from a recession.

Bond funds are just a mutual fund of bonds, and there are many types: treasury bond funds, municipal bond funds, corporate bond funds, high yield (or junk) bond funds, international bond funds, etcetera. Bond funds allow smaller investors to buy into many different bonds. If you can afford to buy many different bonds, then you could avoid the fund fees by buying the bonds instead of a bond fund.

Annuities

If all of these investment options are not enough, there are also money market funds, certificates of deposits and annuities. An annuity is basically an insurance policy that guarantees a lump sum of money will give you a certain level of income. Be careful of insurance salespeople that want to sell you annuities; in most cases it is a good deal for the salespeople and a poor investment for you. Is the cost of buying an annuity worth it to you to get a guaranteed income? When you have enough money to buy an annuity, you should have enough to invest and create your own income. Is having a guarantee from someone worth the extra cost of paying the insurance company and the agent? You are paying for the guarantee of the annuity, and the only one standing behind that guarantee is the insurance company. If you are interested in annuities, you need to look into how sound the insurance company is that is guaranteeing the annuity.

One of the problems with annuities is that you end up locked into them because of the heavy penalties for withdrawing your money. There are a few cases where annuities could be a wise investment, but I don't like the thought of being locked into an investment. Index annuities will limit your risk when the index goes down, but they also limit your gains when the index goes up. Is the limit on your risk (the downturn) worth the limit on your upside potential (gain)? If you do not want downside risk, then an index annuity may be right for you, but you will pay quite a price in lost growth.

I am not really an advocate for insurance. Insurance has its purpose, but how much do you need? The amount of insurance that is right for you depends on your risk tolerance. Insurance costs you money, so is the peace of mind worth the cost to you? It is your choice how much risk you are comfortable with, but be careful about trying to insure against everything and spending all of your money on insurance.

Can There Be Too Many Investments?

It is always nice to have a lot of investments, but all of the available investment options can be confusing. All of the investment choices can make it hard to make the choice about how you will invest. There are many wise ways to invest, and having so many choices can lead to confusion. I have known people that are so worried about making mistakes that they cannot make a decision and end up making the mistake of not doing anything. I know that it is a wise choice to start spending less than you earn and to begin investing the difference. I do not recommend any particular investment. Do you really need to make the *best* investment choice or is making a *good* investment choice enough? It will be best if you invest wisely for as long as you can, but until time passes, how will you know what is the wisest investment?

Asset Allocation

Asset allocation is just a fancy way of saying how you spread your investment money around. It is how much of your wealth that you have in which types of assets. Such as how much of your portfolio you put in riskier stocks and how much you put in safer bonds. Investments will go up and down. The allocation plan for your investments should allow you to stay calm and stick to your plan.

There is one thing about asset allocation that I find odd. The conventional wisdom is that you should have 5 percent to 10 percent in liquid assets (such as cash, gold, etcetera), 25 percent to 33 percent in real estate, 40 percent in bonds and 60 percent in stocks. This adds up to 130 percent to 143 percent, which is even harder than giving 110 percent. Now some of you are saying that you really hate math. You might even be thinking that conventional wisdom is trying to make it more confusing. Either someone is really bad at math or the different groups are not talking with each other. Really, they are talking about it from different directions. A quarter to a third is conventional wisdom for your housing expense. The split between bonds and stocks is from what you have left for investing after taking care of expenses. Since it has to add up to 100 percent, you could look at conventional wisdom as being that you should have 5 percent to 10 percent in cash or gold, 25 percent to 33 percent in real estate, 34 percent to 42 percent stocks and 23 percent to 28 percent in bonds. Conventional wisdom is not always right, but it is a good place to start.

Conventional wisdom for the allocation ratio between stock (riskier investments) and bonds (less risky investments) would be to have 60 percent stocks and 40 percent bonds, but anywhere from 60 percent stocks and 40 percent bonds to 40 percent stocks and 60 percent bonds would be reasonable, depending on your risk tolerance. Even 70 percent stocks and 30 percent bonds could be acceptable, but it would be abnormally risky. When determining your ratio of stocks to bonds, you could include your cash and gold with your bonds, but I like to keep it simple and just keep cash separate, which is what is normal.

Following the conventional wisdom for asset allocation is a good place to start. You do not need to stick too closely to it, but if you deviate very much, you should make sure that you understand why. Just because a ratio of stocks and bonds is normal does not mean that you have to use that ratio. When returns on investments are low, people often take risks. If you go all in on high yield bonds and penny stocks, you should be aware that you are taking higher risks. If you put all of your money in savings accounts to avoid risk, you should realize that you may miss some money-making opportunities. If someone recommends some distribution of assets that is really abnormal, then you should look into how much money they are making by selling you those assets.

Erin talked Bobby into putting all of their investments in stocks and having some of it in international stocks. Erin wanted to be an aggressive investor and wanted to get the highest return possible on their investments. Bobby did talk Erin into using low-cost index funds to diversify and save on commissions. When the first market correction came, their portfolio took quite a loss. Bobby was then able to talk Erin into putting 30 percent of their investments into corporate bond funds for lower risk, but Erin still wanted 70 percent in stock funds for higher returns. They still had a high-risk portfolio for a higher rate of return, but the risk was reduced a little through diversification. They managed to work together and came to a compromise that was not as aggressive as Erin wanted nor as safe as Bobby may have wanted either, but for them it was a wise investment plan.

Allocations Based on Age

When you invest, ask yourself when you will want your money. If you will want the money soon, then savings accounts, certificates of deposit, and money markets would be wise investments because you can withdraw your money without significant cost. If you can invest the money for a few years or more, then real estate and stocks would be wise investments. The price of real estate and stocks can be volatile so you may have to wait for their value to increase.

Over the long run stocks have better returns than bonds, but at any time stocks can lose money. When you are young, you have more time to recover from any down turn in the stock market. So the standard advice is to invest more heavily in stocks when you are young and more heavily in bonds when you are older. The standard ratio for investment allocation is 60 percent stocks and 40 percent bonds when you are young and 40 percent stocks and 60 percent bonds as you get old. So, when are you considered old? The standard is you are getting old as you approach retirement. I would say that you are getting old as you approach the end of your life expectancy, however, this makes it difficult to determine when you are getting old because you do not know if you will live to 80 or if you might live to 100. If you are married, you should also account for your spouse's life expectancy. These factors make it less certain as to when you should switch the ratio of stocks and bonds. If you are healthy, I would recommend erring on the side of staying with stocks longer.

There are funds that will adjust the ratio of stocks to bonds as you get older. These life cycle funds are designed to make life time balancing easier, and I have nothing against easy. You should know that they assume you'll want a safer portfolio as you grow older, and they assume what is old for you. This would also assume that you have all of your portfolio in one fund, when what matters is the balance of your entire portfolio.

Rebalance to Stick with Your Allocation

Sticking with your allocation is important, which is easier when using a fixed ratio like 60 percent stocks and 40 percent bonds. I like easy because I can stick with it, which could be more important than what allocation you use. Stock and bond values will change, so the amount of stocks and bonds will need to be changed in order to stick with a fixed ratio. How often you rebalance your portfolio is up to you, but the more often that you rebalance your portfolio, the more that you will pay in fees. Spending a lot of time rebalancing your portfolio ensures that you spend a lot on fees.

Since there is nothing magical about any particular fixed ratio, I would recommend you only rebalance a couple of times a year. To maintain the ratio of stocks and bonds that you want, I like buying the ones that I want more of instead of selling the ones that I want less of. If you can, I would recommend only selling when you need the money, such as for retirement, and then selling the ones that you want less of. When you can, avoid *both* buying and selling to get the ratio of stocks and bonds that you want, since this would just increase your transaction fees. Why make more trades and pay more commissions than you have to?

Picking Stocks

There are people that enjoy picking stocks. Many people like to think that they can pick stocks better than others can. It is unlikely that you would be able to get as much information about the market as the institutional investors that spend millions on market research. If the excitement of picking your own stocks is worth the potential loss, then enjoy and good luck.

Some love to research and track stocks, and there is nothing wrong with that, but I am not convinced that all that effort pays off enough to balance out the cost of all of the time that it takes. Personally, I am lazy and do not want to research stocks. I have done all right with index funds and mutual funds. I do not know if I could have done better with individual stocks, but I do know that I would have spent a lot of my time trying to figure out which were the good stocks and which were the bad stocks. Just because I do not want to take the risk of picking individual stocks does not mean that it is not a wise investment for you if you are comfortable with the risk. For those that like the challenge of researching and trying to pick the winning stock, go ahead and have some fun. The odds of picking good stocks are better than trying to pick the winning horse at the race track. If picking stocks is not for you and it is just stressful, then why bother unless it is just to make larger commissions for your stock broker or financial advisor.

Value investors buy stocks that have a low price relative to the book value of the company. To look at how companies are valued, look at this book's appendix on applying the Equation for Wealth beyond individuals. In the long run value investing is not a bad strategy, but there is no perfect strategy, and you may not want to wait for the long run. There have been times when both growth stocks and the main index have done better than value investing. At any moment the stock market does not have to go in the same direction as the underlining companies. When the companies are doing well, then the stock market should do well, eventually. Eventually the stock market should reflect the value of the companies that make up the market. The small investor should not expect to be able to time when the market will reflect the value of the underlining companies. If there was a way to time the market, then many investors would, and they in turn, would be affecting the timing of the market.

Dollar Cost Averaging

Dollar cost averaging is a strategy that is easy to use. Dollar cost averaging is simply investing the same amount at regular intervals, such as investing $100 a month into a stock fund, whether the stock is going up or going down. Some would argue that it may not be the best strategy, but it is a good strategy. It is a strategy that can be used when buying stocks, mutual funds or bonds. When the stock is down, you buy more stocks then when the stock is up, but you are always investing the same amount. So you end up buying low without trying to time the bottom of the market (when the market is at its lowest point).

Your Wise Investment

Is it best to buy stocks that are selling for less than the book value of the company, to follow the momentum of the market, or to not try to time the market? Buying low and selling high is a wise strategy, but it can be hard to do.

The simplest strategy is to pick the allocation of your assets and stick to it. The simplest strategy does not require frequent trades, so it reduces trading costs, and it also reduces your chance of making a costly mistake. The simplest strategy may not turn out to be the most profitable strategy, but I like to keep things simple. What I like may not be best for you. If you can accept the risk of chasing after a strategy that might be more profitable and you enjoy the chase, then that might be best for you. Over time you will find out if it truly was a wise investment. Investing wisely should take into account your goals and your risk tolerance. This is where the Equation for Wealth would come in handy. You can use the Equation for Wealth to see what rate of return and therefore what level of risk is needed to meet your goals, or you can use the level of risk that you are comfortable with to see what goals you can reach.

There are some investments that most people would agree to be unwise investment. Almost everyone would agree that lottery tickets and fishing boats are unwise investments. That may not stop you from buying them, just don't bother calling them investments because people will think you are crazy or at best they will laugh and not believe you.

Time

There is little reason to think about what could have been if we had made other choices in the past. Although we often dwell on the past, it only leads to regrets. We are not able to go back in time to change the choices that we made. We are also not really able to know what would have happened if we had made other choices. We can only imagine what could have been, and what we imagine is really nothing more than our dreams. There is not much that you can do about the mistakes of the past except to learn from them, so that you can avoid making the same mistakes in the future. We can learn lessons from the past, but how do you invest based on the past? Mortgage backed securities caused the stock market and real estate to crash in 2008 but that does not mean that you should avoid investing in stocks and real estate. Even the past is not a sure thing. We cannot even agree about what the past was as we argue about what lessons we should learn from the past.

You will find that higher returns in early years and higher asset acquisition in early years will have a disproportionate effect on the growth of your wealth. So if you can do well in your younger years, you will have more wealth in your later years. Of course, if you could, you probably would want to do well throughout all of your years. Like most of us, in my younger years I was just trying to get by the best that I could. There really is not much that we can do about when we do well, except to always try to do the best that we can. All that you can do is to make the most of the time that you have. You can focus on the mistakes you made in the past and complain that there is not enough time left, or you can move on and make the best of the time that you have.

Time is very important to successful investing. The more time that you have, the longer your investments can grow and the greater the wealth you will be able to obtain. One of the few things that you can do to effect time is to procrastinate and put off saving and investing. If you have made the mistake of putting off saving and investing, then fix that mistake by beginning to save and invest now. Starting to save early gives more time for your money to grow. Yesterday would be a good time to start saving, but if you didn't, then today is the best day to start spending less then you earn so that you can invest what you have saved. You will never have more time than you do now. There is no point in lamenting that you could have started earlier. All you can do is to start now and make the best of the time that you have. Automatically saving a portion of your earnings ensures that you will save something. It is a good start and starting to save can be the hardest part of saving and investing. See chapter 6 "If It's Simple, Why Isn't Everyone Wealthy" and chapter 7 "Other Tips for Success" for more on getting started.

Compounding: Good and Bad

Time compounds the interest on your savings and helps your investments to grow. Compounding interest is making interest on the interest that you have already made. The money you made is working for you and making even more money.

Unfortunately, time also compounds the cost of borrowing money. There is not just compound interest, there is also compounding of the actions that you take. When you consume and spend more today, it means that you did not acquire assets, assets that could have increased in value. What you do when you are young will have a disproportional effect because there is more time to benefit from what you do right or to suffer from your mistakes. You should start saving while you are young so that you can benefit from compounding interest over a longer period of time. Unfortunately, the effects of mistakes are also compounded.

You will not only be paying the cost of the mistake; you will also have the opportunity cost of not benefitting from what you could have done.

Prepared for the Future?

Saving enough can be very difficult. We would rather spend today than invest for our uncertain future needs. You will not really know what you'll need until the future, but you will need to estimate what you'll need in order to be able to determine how much you need to save today. Many people underestimate how much they will need to meet their long-term needs. How do you determine the value of saving for your needs in an uncertain future? Will what you forgo today in order to save be worth it in the future? We tend to place too much value on the present enjoyment from spending and fail to account for the cost in the future. It is impossible to predict the future with certainty, but many financial problems come from being unwilling to consider our future needs until they have become a crisis. So many are unprepared for their future needs, such as retirement, when they do eventually come. There are retirement calculators on the internet that will help you determine what you will need for retirement but many of them are advertisement for investments that they want to sell you, so be carefully. You could use the Equation for Wealth to determine how much wealth you could build for retirement.

Chapter 4

First Step of the Mathematical Equation for Wealth

The Equation for Wealth begins with what your wealth would be for one time period, such as what happens to your wealth today or this year. If the period of time is very small such as a minute or a second, then it basically becomes this moment in time. We will start with understanding what happens to wealth in one period of time before we move on to multiple periods of time.

How much wealth you will have after a period of time is pretty simple to calculate. It is how much wealth you started with, plus how much that wealth grew (return on investment) during that period of time, plus how much more wealth you added (new assets minus new liabilities) during that period of time. There should be nothing surprising in this.

This book is based on an equation, so you know that we were going to get to some math sometime. Math is just one way to describe something. The information in this book is presented in different ways (math, graphs, descriptions) so if one way of presenting the information (such as math) does not work for you, then skim through it and learn the concepts from the other ways (such as graphs and written descriptions).

You do not need to understand all of the math but you may want to follow along so that you understand the basics of the equation. I'll walk you through the math and strive to make it easy for you to follow. If you really dislike math, do not be discouraged; you can still understand the principles, even if you ignore the math as you read through this chapter and the next chapter. For those that do skim through all of the math, I think that it would be worthwhile to come back to it later and follow along with the description of the equation. Skimming at first and then coming back and reading it again can help you to understand the equation and you may find that it is not as complicated as it may look like at first. Alternatively, you could find someone that does like math to help you through the portions that you may have trouble with.

So follow as much or as little of the math as you like. Do not let any difficulty understanding the details of the mathematical Equation for Wealth stop you from understanding the Formula for Wealth (spend less than you earn and invest the difference wisely for as long as you can). Let the mathematical Equation for Wealth show you the truth behind the Formula for Wealth. You do not need to apply the math of the

Equation for Wealth to be able to apply the Formula for Wealth to your life.

Mathematically, with your net worth being the measure of your wealth, there is one path toward greater wealth, which is to increase your net worth. (You can review net worth in Chapter 1 "So, What is Monetary Wealth?" if you want to.) How much wealth you will have after a period of time would be your net worth, and we will call this NW_1. The net worth that you will have after a period of time would be the assets that you started with minus the liabilities that you started with plus the return on those assets plus the assets that you acquired minus the liabilities that you acquired. I will walk you through this step by step. As an equation, it would look like this:

$Net\ Worth_1$ = $Assets_0$ - $Liabilities_0$ + Return on $Investment_1$ x $Assets_0$ - Return on $Investment_1$ x $Liabilities_0$ + $Assets_1$ - $Liabilities_1$. Which could also be written as $Net\ Worth_1$ = $Assets_0$ - $Liabilities_0$ + Return on $Investment_1$ x ($Assets_0$ - $Liabilities_0$) + $Assets_1$ - $Liabilities_1$. (The subscript numbers refer to the associated time period.)

It could also be written as follows:

$$NW_1 = A_0 - L_0 + ROI_1 \times A_0 - ROI_1 \times L_0 + A_1 - L_1$$

Which could also be written as

$$NW_1 = A_0 - L_0 + ROI_1(A_0 - L_0) + A_1 - L_1$$

With 1 being an increment of time since time 0

NW_1 being your net worth after time period 1

A_0 being your initial assets

L_0 being your initial liabilities

ROI_1 being the return on investment during time period 1

A_1 being the assets acquired during time period 1

L_1 being the liabilities incurred during time period 1

Initial net worth is initial assets minus initial liabilities or $NW_0 = A_0 - L_0$. So we can simplify it a bit further by replacing $A_0 - L_0$ with NW_0 and it can then be written like this:

$$NW_1 = NW_0 + (ROI_1)NW_0 + A_1 - L_1$$

Let us look at Alex before he started college. He was highly motivated early on and got a job in high school to help get prepared for engineering school. He finished his junior year in high school with no debt and $5,000 in a savings account, so his initial net worth (NW_0) is $5,000. His savings account paid an annual interest rate of 5 percent. Expressed as a decimal ROI_1 is 0.05. Alex continued to spend less than he earned, and during this year he saved $2,000. So, this year the difference between assets (A_1) and liabilities (L_1) is $2,000.

Putting these numbers into $NW_1 = NW_0 + (ROI_1)$ $NW_0 + A_1 - L_1$ we would have

$$NW_1 = \$5,000 + (0.05)\$5,000 + \$2,000 \text{ so}$$

$$NW_1 = \$5,000 + \$250 + \$2,000 = \$7,250$$

After a year, Alex's net worth (NW_1) has grown to \$7,250, and he can graduate high school with a good financial start towards his first year of college.

This equation is just another way of saying, the wealth after a period of time is how much you started with plus how much that grew plus how much wealth you made during that period of time. How much wealth you start with would be your initial net worth, and we will represent it as NW_0. How much your initial wealth grew during the period of time is your initial net worth times the rate of return on its investment and we will represent it this way: (Return on Investment$_1$) x (Assets$_0$ - Liabilities$_0$) or (ROI_1) NW_0. If we assume your assets are purchased from the income that you have left after your spending, then how much wealth you made during the period of time would be the difference between what you earned and what you spent.

Whatever period of time you use whether it is this second, this minute, this day or this year; your net worth for this period of time is $NW_1 = NW_0 + (ROI_1)$ $NW_0 + A_1 - L_1$. When you put this into words it would be; net worth after a period of time (NW_1) is equal to initial net worth (NW_0) plus the return on initial net worth $[(ROI_1)NW_0]$ plus the assets from that period (A_1) minus the liabilities from that period (L_1).

All of these symbols may look intimidating, but you do not need to be good at math to use the Equation for Wealth. When the math is more than you want to deal with, then just move past it. You can always come back to the math if you wish. You can rely on the descriptions and examples to understand the Equation for Wealth. Seeing the math may help you to have confidence in the descriptions and examples.

You could also look at assets minus liabilities as income minus expenses. This is not quite true, but most of the time we acquire assets and liabilities by the difference between our income and expenses. I want to encourage you to spend less than you earn, so I will often use the simplifying assumption that income minus expenses is approximately assets minus liabilities.

There are only a few factors to the Equation for Wealth and only a few of them that you can control. The easiest way to get a small fortune is to start with a large fortune, but there is not much you can do about what your initial wealth is. You were able to make choices in the past that effect your current net worth, but you cannot go back in time to change any of those past choices. The three factors that you can work on now are the rate of return on your investments, your income and your spending.

Let's say that you started with nothing, then initial net worth is nothing or $NW_0 = 0$ and the equation

$$NW_1 = NW_0 + (ROI_1)NW_0 + A_1 - L_1$$
$$\ldots \text{becomes } NW_1 = 0 + (ROI_1)0 + A_1 - L_1$$

Which is just $NW_1 = A_1 - L_1$

This is just the mathematical way of saying that you started with nothing, so you had nothing to invest and your net worth is the assets you acquired minus the liabilities that you acquired during this period of time. This is as simple as the equation gets, but this is not very often likely to be reality.

Almost everyone has something other than zero for their net worth. There are some people who have just a little net worth and would like more. While others have too much debt and would like to get their net worth up to zero.

Let us look at the following example of Bobby and Erin's early years together. They made $50,000 a year, but up to that point they had been spending even more, so that they had a debt of $15,000 ($NW_0$). It is too bad they didn't have this book, but they did find one that helped them decide to get their spending under control and spend less than they earned so that they could invest the difference in paying off their debt. They had a combined essential yearly expense (taxes, food, utilities, rent, etcetera) of $40,000 and $10,000 ($A_1 - L_1$) a year of income that they could use to purchase assets without taking on any more liabilities. So, using this example, Net Worth equals Initial Net Worth plus Return On Investment times Initial Net Worth plus Assets minus Liabilities:

$$NW_1 = NW_0 + (ROI_1)NW_0 + A_1 - L_1 \text{ becomes}$$

$$NW_1 = -\$15,000 + (ROI_1)(-\$15,000) + \$10,000$$

when we put in the initial net worth NW_0 of -\$15,000 with earnings of \$50,000 and spending of \$40,000, which means assets minus liabilities acquired during time period 1 ($A_1 - L_1$) would be \$10,000.

Since I like round numbers, let's say that the interest rate on their debt was 10 percent a year. The percentage would be expressed as a decimal and ROI_1 would be 0.10. So their net worth ($NW_1 = NW_0 + (ROI_1)NW_0 + A_1 - L_1$) after one year would be -\$6,500.

$$NW_1 = -\$15,000 + (0.10)(-\$15,000) + \$10,000 = -\$6,500.$$

They were not able to pay off their debt in the first year, so they still had a net worth that was negative. They could also have tried to borrow more money to invest in something that they thought would have a greater return than the interest on their debt. If they did that, they would have been taking a big risk since the return they were likely to make on their investment was unlikely to be as high as the interest on their debt, which would result in an even larger negative net worth. Instead of trying to invest their way out of debt, Bobby and Erin chose the wiser option of paying off as much of their debt as they could that year and then continued to pay off their debt the next year. It may have taken them a couple of years to pay off all of their debt, but by keeping at it they were successful. For more on paying off debt see chapter 7 "Other Tips for Success."

Normally, paying off as much of your debt as you can is the best that you can do to increase your net worth. Bobby and Erin got their new jobs with better benefits and their new employer matched 5 percent of their income [$50,000(0.05) = $2,500] that they put into their retirement accounts. (It is a good idea to take all of the benefits that your employer is giving out.) The best thing for them to do was to take the free money their employer was giving out by investing $2,500 into their retirement accounts and use the remaining ($10,000 - $2,500 = $7,500) to pay off debt.

Let's put these new figures into the equation for net worth after one year. Net worth equals initial net worth plus return on investment times initial net worth plus assets minus liabilities. Or written as an equation, it looks like this:

$$NW_1 = NW_0 + (ROI_1)NW_0 + A_1 - L_1$$

When initial net worth NW_0 is -$15,000, interest rate on their debt was 10 percent a year (so ROI_1

= 0.10) and earnings are $50,000 and spending is $40,000, which means assets minus liabilities acquired during time period 1 (A_1 - L_1) would be $10,000 plus the matching contribution of $2,500, the equation would look like this:

$$NW_1 = -\$15,000 + (0.10)(-\$15,000) + \$10,000 + \$2,500$$
(matching contribution) = -$4,000

After one year, their net worth would be -$4,000. They may have still had some debt to pay off next year, but their employer had given them an extra $2,500 in their retirement account that year so their net worth increased by the amount of that asset. Their net worth was still negative, but not as negative as it was without the extra $2,500 that their employer gave them.

This is the only example that I can think of where delaying paying off your debt could make sense. When your employer does not match your contribution to your retirement account, it would be better to pay off as much debt as you can, but starting a retirement account as soon as practical would still be wise.

We would probably all prefer to start with a lot of money instead of being in debt. Wouldn't you have liked to start this time period by winning the lottery? Let's say that you did win the lottery, and you are starting with two million dollars after taxes. So, your initial net worth is NW_0 = $2,000,000. The financial advisor (see chapter 7 "Other Tips for Success") that you hired manages to make 10 percent on your investments, so your return on investment (ROI_1) is 0.10. You quit your job and splurge on some of the things that you always wanted. You start by buying a million-dollar home. This would be an asset, and it would just be changing one asset (cash) for another asset (real estate). Of course, there are expenses when buying real estate so it would not be a straight conversion of cash to real estate. If you want to be more accurate, you could subtract the cost of the transaction from buying the asset, but I don't want to complicate this too much.

To make things easier let's say that you bought the house after you invested. So, for this example it does not affect what your financial advisor had available to invest. You also take on liabilities of paying your financial advisor $50,000 a year and your new accountant $50,000 a year. Let's assume you only go a little crazy with your spending and you blow $150,000 on living and having a good time. Your liabilities for the year would be L_1 = $50,000 + $50,000 + $150,000 = $250,000. So, after one year your net worth equals initial net worth plus return on investment times initial net worth plus assets minus liabilities or $NW_1 = NW_0 +$ $(ROI_1)NW_0 + A_1 - L_1$ would look like this when we put in the numbers (NW_0 of $2,000,000, ROI_1 of 0.10 and L_1 of $250,000):

$$NW_1 = \$2,000,000 + (0.10)(\$2,000,000) - \$250,000$$
$$= \$1,950,000.$$

Even without working anymore your investment income made up for most of your spending. If you could keep your spending close to or below the return on your investment $[(ROI_1)NW_0]$, you could then win $2,000,000 in the lottery and retire. It would be nice to start out with winning the lottery, but your odds are against it.

Don't worry if you didn't like the math in the Equation for Wealth. In the next chapter we will go through various examples for applying the Equation for Wealth. I will provide graphs and descriptions to help explain the examples. Understanding the application of the equation is more important than going through the math of the equation.

Chapter 5

The Mathematical Equation
for Wealth

I am hoping that I have done a good job of explaining the Equation for Wealth so far because now we are going to add to its complexity by adding in the effect of multiple increments of time. The mathematical Equation for Wealth does not care what increments you use for time as long as you are consistent and use the same increment throughout the equation. As the increment of time gets smaller, the accuracy of the equation gets greater. Going from years to days to hours to seconds would progressively give you a more accurate outcome. The increments that you use need to be the same throughout the equation, including your forecast for the return on your investment. Would your forecast for the rate of return be accurate, an estimate or just a close guess? If your return on investment is an approximation, then how precise does the rest of your calculation really need to be?

After each increment of time, your new level of wealth is how much wealth you had plus how much it grew plus how many assets you gained minus how many liabilities you added. Using a day as the increment of time, then the Equation for Wealth is as follows:

The wealth you'll have at the end of today is the wealth you had yesterday plus how much it grew today plus the wealth that you acquire today.

You might be thinking if it is that simple, why did I spend money on this book. Well, sorry, no refund. This book is an asset that you bought yesterday and the return you make on that investment today will help determine your wealth tomorrow.

The increment of time could be small, such as daily. In which case the rate of return on investments also has to be daily. Do not let the math of compounding daily confuse the general concepts of the Equation for Wealth. The principle stays the same, and while accuracy is gained by using a day as the increment of time in your calculation, little is gained in understanding. So we will be using years for the time increments and yearly rates of return on investments. If the math gets hard to follow, then just stay focused on the principles.

Symbol for Summation

Before we get to the Equation for Wealth, I would like to review or introduce you to a mathematical symbol for summation (capital sigma notation). You will not need to know any calculus but I want you to recognize the symbol when you see it. I will make this easier for you to follow when we get to the Equation for Wealth.

$$\text{The symbol } \sum_{i=m}^{n} \text{ means}$$

To replace i in what is after the symbol with the whole numbers from m to n and then add them all together.

Such as . . .

$$\sum_{i=m}^{n} a_i = a_m + a_{m+1} + a_{m+2} + a_{m+3} \ldots + a_n$$

An example would be . . .

$$\sum_{i=1}^{5} i = 1 + 2 + 3 + 4 + 5 = 15$$

An example more applicable to wealth would be assets minus liabilities for three years which would be written as the following equation:

$$\sum_{i=1}^{3} (A_i - L_i) = (A_1 - L_1) + (A_2 - L_2) + (A_3 - L_3)$$

Where A_i is the assets acquired during time period i. L_i is the liabilities acquired during time period i.

This equation may look really difficult, but it is really not that difficult. This is just a fancy way of saying assets minus liabilities $(A_i - L_i)$ repeated for each time period and then added together.

A_1, A_2 and A_3 do not need to be the same and L_1, L_2 and L_3 do not need to be the same.

To have a few numbers to use let's say that $A_1 = \$1,000$, $A_2 = \$4,000$, $A_3 = \$6,000$, $L_1 = \$500$, $L_2 = \$1,000$ and $L_3 = \$2,000$. Putting these number into the equation we get the following:

$$\sum_{i=1}^{3} (A_i - L_i) = (A_1 - L_1) + (A_2 - L_2) + (A_3 - L_3)$$

$$= (\$1,000 - \$500) + (\$4,000 - \$1,000) + (\$6,000 - \$2,000)$$

$$= \$500 + \$3,000 + \$4,000$$

$$= \$7,500$$

In this example you would have added \$7,500 more in assets than liabilities over a three-year period. This is not the Equation for Wealth because we did not include the wealth that we started with or the return on investing our wealth.

We will need to combine the equation $(NW_1 = NW_0 + (ROI_1)NW_0 + A_1 - L_1)$ from chapter 4 "First Step of the Mathematical Equation for Wealth" with the symbol for summation to get the Equation for Wealth.

The Equation for Wealth

So here is the Equation for Wealth:

$$NW_n = NW_0 + \sum_{i=1}^{n} [ROI_i(NW_{i-1}) + A_i - L_i]$$

Where NW_n is the net worth at the end of time period n

NW_0 is initial net worth

NW_{i-1} is the net worth at time period i minus 1

ROI_i is the return on investment during time period i

A_i is the assets acquired during time period i

L_i is the liabilities acquired during time period i

Remember that i will be replaced with each time period from 1 to n, and then all of the time periods are added together.

This equation may look really difficult, but it is really not that difficult. This is just a fancy way of saying that the Equation for Wealth is ($NW_1 = NW_0 + (ROI_1)$ $NW_0 + A_1 - L_1$) repeated for every period of time and added together until you reach the end.

You will not have to solve the Equation for Wealth for yourself. I will provide examples and their solutions so that you can follow as much of the math as you wish and still understand how the Equation for Wealth can be applied to you.

There is a way to solve this equation that is so easy that it is boring and tedious.

$$NW_n = NW_0 + \sum_{i=1}^{n} [ROI_i(NW_{i-1}) + A_i - L_i]$$

After one time period, it would be . . .

$$NW_1 = NW_0 + (ROI_1)NW_0 + A_1 - L_1.$$

After two time periods it would become $NW_2 = NW_0 + (ROI_1)NW_0 + A_1 - L_1 + (ROI_2)NW_1 + A_2 - L_2$. Remembering that $NW_0 + (ROI_1)NW_0 + A_1 - L_1 = NW_1$ we can replace $NW_0 + (ROI_1)NW_0 + A_1 - L_1$ with NW_1 in the equation to get $NW_2 = NW_1 + (ROI_2)NW_1 + A_2 - L_2$. Notice that this is very similar to what we had for the first time period. So you can solve the second time period if you take what you got in the first time period and put it into the next.

You can then continue to take what you get from one time period and put it into the next until you get to the last time period. So all you are really doing is using $NW + (ROI)NW + A - L$ over and over again until you have solved the problem.

When you determine how much wealth you want, then you can use the Equation for Wealth to calculate how much you need to invest, the return on investment that you need and how long it would take to get the wealth that you desire.

The First Few Steps

Your net worth could be seen as the equation for your wealth at this current period of time. The Equation for Wealth could be looked at as your current net worth plus the change in your net worth in the future. The Equation for Wealth could be seen as how much you started with, plus how much that has changed and how much more you have obtained.

This is a little simplistic, so we will have to make it more complex to be useful. The Equation for Wealth is your initial net worth plus the rate of return on your initial net worth plus how much you added to your initial net worth, and this is repeated for as many time periods as you want.

You remember the first step of the Equation for Wealth; net worth equals initial net worth plus return on initial net worth plus added assets minus additional liabilities over a certain period of time.

$$NW_1 = NW_0 + (ROI_1)NW_0 + A_1 - L_1.$$

Now we have to add in the second period of time. The wealth after a period of time is how much you started that period of time with plus how much that grew plus how much wealth you made during that period of time.

The equation after the second period of time is very similar to the equation for the first period of time. The equation after the second period of time looks like this:

$$NW_2 = NW_0 + \sum_{i=1}^{2} [ROI_i(NW_{i-1}) + A_i - L_i]$$

And would become . . .

$$NW_2 = NW_0 + (ROI_1)NW_0 + A_1 - L_1 + (ROI_2)NW_1 + A_2 - L_2.$$

Placing what we had gotten from first time period $(NW_1 = NW_0 + (ROI_1)NW_0 + A_1 - L_1)$ into the equation for the second period of time allows it to be written as:

$$NW_2 = NW_1 + (ROI_2)NW_1 + A_2 - L_2.$$

The wealth after the next period of time (NW_2) is how much you started with at the beginning of that period of time (NW_1) plus how much that grew $[(ROI_2)NW_1]$ plus how much wealth you made during that period of time $(A_2 - L_2)$.

It is getting a little more complicated, but it is really just the same equation repeated for two periods of time.

The third step is again very similar.

$$NW_3 = NW_0 + \sum_{i=1}^{3} [ROI_i(NW_{i-1}) + A_i - L_i]$$

And would become . . .

$$NW_3 = NW_0 + (ROI_1)NW_0 + A_1 - L_1 + (ROI_2)NW_1 + A_2 - L_2 + (ROI_3)NW_2 + A_3 - L_3.$$

Placing what we had gotten from the second time period $(NW_0 + (ROI_1)NW_0 + A_1 - L_1 + (ROI_2)NW_1 + A_2 - L_2)$ into the equation for the third period of time allows it to be written as:

$$NW_3 = NW_2 + (ROI_3)NW_2 + A_3 - L_3.$$

I hope that you are seeing a pattern. This pattern would then go on for as many periods of time as you had. The description would be similar to the second step, but longer.

Formula for Wealth

We start with the Equation for Wealth.

$$NW_n = NW_0 + \sum_{i=1}^{n} [ROI_i(NW_{i-1}) + A_i - L_i]$$

Then we assume that for most of us, we acquire assets or liabilities from the difference between what we earn and what we spend. The Formula for Wealth is to spend less than you earn and invest the difference wisely for as long as you can. The Formula for Wealth takes an equation that most of us would not want to use and makes an assumption that is true for most of us, in order to simplify the equation to a sentence that we can easily use.

There are three factors to the Formula for Wealth: (1) spend less than you earn, (2) invest the difference wisely, (3) for as long as you can. If you forecast two of the three, then you can calculate the third.

When you are following a budget, you know what the difference is between what you spend and what you earn (1). Then you forecast one of two other parameters: either what the return on investment will be (2) or what the length of time will be (3). Once you decide what parameter you are forecasting, then you can calculate what the other parameter will need to be to reach your goal. I will use the next few scenarios to illustrate some of the main points through the Equation for Wealth.

Example Using the Equation for Wealth with High Income

Blair came from a middle-class family and went to nursing school after high school. Blair worked as a nurse for a while to build up funds for medical school. While in medical school Blair fell in love with a law student named Frankie. Between classes and studying, they did not have much time for each other while in school, but they got married shortly after graduation. After graduating, they got good paying jobs, and they were doing quite well financially. Their biggest worry was whether they were spoiling their children as they took them on European vacations and bought them new cars. They got curious as to how long it would take them to reach their goal of becoming millionaires. We can use their budget at this time of their lives for the difference between what they spend and what they earn, forecast what they can earn on their investments and then we will calculate when they can reach their goal of being millionaires.

The following examples are intentionally simplified to limit how much is changing at one time, in order to see the effect of one or two things. In reality many things could be changing, and this can make it hard to see the effect of any particular change. The rate of return on investment (ROI), the assets acquired (A) and the liabilities acquired (L) could change every year, but for clarity I will not be changing them from year to year in these examples.

For our fictional couple Blair and Frankie, who are making a good income, their budget is to spend $50,000 a year less than they earn (A - L = $50,000), and we forecast that they can earn 10 percent return on their investment (ROI = 0.1), and I calculated that they would be millionaires in less than 12 years, even if they started with nothing ($NW_0 = 0$).

I am using 10 percent return on investment because I like round numbers, and all you will need to do is to move the decimal place. It is possible (and probable) to have a different return on your investment each year, which would complicate the math, so I am applying an average and using it for each year. Also, 10 percent would work as a reasonable average forecast for the yearly return on investment.

By putting in the number that you get for net worth from one step and then putting it into the next step, working through the Equation for Wealth for this example would be as follows:

$$NW_n = NW_0 + \sum_{i=1}^{n} [ROI_i(NW_{i-1}) + A_i - L_i]$$

Putting in our forecast for ROI of 0.1 and the $50,000 (A - L) that their budget says they are able to invest, then we solve for how long it will take to reach their goal when they start with nothing ($NW_0 = 0$).

$$NW_n = 0 + \sum_{i=1}^{n} [0.1(NW_{i-1}) + \$50,000]$$

And we solve for n when $NW_n > \$1,000,000$

I will use the summation a few times so that you are introduced to it and so that you can see the transition from the summation to the easy way to solve the problem.

We can solve this by using NW + (ROI)NW + A - L over and over again until we have solved the problem. We continue to take what we get from one time period and put it into the next time period until you get to the last time period.

Net worth after one year equals initial net worth plus return on initial net worth plus added assets minus additional liabilities.

$$NW_1 = NW_0 + (ROI_1)NW_0 + A_1 - L_1 = 0 + \$50,000$$

The net worth after the first year would be $50,000.

Take the number that you got for net worth in the first step ($50,000) and put it into the second step.

$$NW_2 = NW_1 + (ROI_2)NW_1 + A_2 - L_2.$$
$$NW_2 = \$50,000 + (0.1)\$50,000 + \$50,000 =$$
$\$50,000 + \$5,000 + \$50,000 = \$105,000$

After the second year, the net worth is $105,000.

Take the number that you got for net worth in the second step ($105,000) and put it into the third step.

$$NW_3 = NW_2 + (ROI_3)NW_2 + A_3 - L_3.$$
$$NW_3 = \$105,000 + (0.1)\$105,000 + \$50,000 =$$
$\$105,000 + \$10,500 + \$50,000 = \$165,500$

After the third year, the net worth is $165,500.

This gets repetitive so feel free to skim to the end of the problem.

Take the number that you got for net worth in the third step ($165,500) and put it into the fourth step.

$$NW_4 = NW_3 + (ROI_4)NW_3 + A_4 - L_4.$$
$$NW_4 = \$165,500 + (0.1)\$165,500 + \$50,000 =$$
$\$165,500 + \$16,550 + \$50,000 = \$232,050$

After the fourth year, the net worth is $232,050.

Take the number that you got for net worth in the fourth step ($232,050) and put it into the fifth step.

$$NW_5 = NW_4 + (ROI_5)NW_4 + A_5 - L_5.$$
$$NW_5 = \$232,050 + (0.1)\$232,050 + \$50,000 =$$
$\$232,050 + \$23,205 + \$50,000 = \$305,255$

After the fifth year, the net worth is $305,255.

Take the number that you got for net worth in the fifth step ($305,255) and put it into the sixth step.

$$NW_6 = NW_5 + (ROI_6)NW_5 + A_6 - L_6.$$

NW_6 = $305,255 + (0.1)$305,255 + $50,000 = $305,255 + $30,526 + $50,000 = $385,781

After the sixth year, the net worth is $385,781.

Take the number that you got for net worth in the sixth step ($385,781) and put it into the seventh step.

$$NW_7 = NW_6 + (ROI_7)NW_6 + A_7 - L_7.$$

NW_7 = $385,781 + (0.1)$385,781 + $50,000 = $385,781 + $38,578 + $50,000 = $474,359

After the seventh year, the net worth is $474,359.

Take the number that you got for net worth in the seventh step ($474,359) and put it into the eighth step.

$$NW_8 = NW_7 + (ROI_8)NW_7 + A_8 - L_8.$$

NW_8 = $474,359 + (0.1)$474,359 + $50,000 = $474,359 + $47,436 + $50,000 = $571,795

After the eighth year, the net worth is $571,795.

Take the number that you got for net worth in the eighth step ($571,795) and put it into the ninth step.

$$NW_9 = NW_8 + (ROI_9)NW_8 + A_9 - L_9.$$

NW_9 = $571,795 + (0.1)$571,795 + $50,000 = $571,795 + $57,180 + $50,000 = $678,975

After the ninth year, the net worth is $678,975.

Take the number that you got for net worth in the ninth step ($678,975) and put it into the tenth step.

$$NW_{10} = NW_9 + (ROI_{10})NW_9 + A_{10} - L_{10.}$$

NW_{10} = \$678,975 + (0.1)\$678,975 + \$50,000 = \$678,975 + \$67,898 + \$50,000 = \$796,873

After the tenth year, the net worth is \$796,873.

Take the number that you got for net worth in the tenth step (\$796,873) and put it into the eleventh step.

$$NW_{11} = NW_{10} + (ROI_{11})NW_{10} + A_{11} - L_{11.}$$

NW_{11} = \$796,873 + (0.1)\$796,873 + \$50,000 = \$796,873 + \$79,687 + \$50,000 = \$926,560

After the eleventh year, the net worth is \$926,560.

Take the number that you got for net worth in the eleventh step (\$926,560) and put it into the twelfth step.

$$NW_{12} = NW_{11} + (ROI_{12})NW_{11} + A_{12} - L_{12.}$$

NW_{12} = \$926,560 + (0.1)\$926,560 + \$50,000 = \$926,560 + \$92,656 + \$50,000 = \$1,069,216

After the twelfth year, the net worth is \$1,069,216.

Example Using the Equation for Wealth with Moderate Income

The second example is our fictional characters Bobby and Erin. They were worried that they would need to become millionaires if they were ever going to be able to retire. We will use the budget from this middle-class couple for the difference between what they spend and what they earn, forecast what they could earn on their investments and then we will calculate when they could reach their goal of being millionaires so that they could retire.

They are not doctors or lawyers, and they find it hard to save, but their budget allows them to save $5,000 a year, and their employer matches their contribution to their retirement accounts (A - L = $10,000). They invest that $10,000 each year and get 10 percent return on their investment (ROI = 0.1), they would be millionaires in less than 26 years, assuming that they started with nothing ($NW_0 = 0$). Again, by putting in the number that you get for net worth from one step and then putting it into the next step, working through the Equation for Wealth for this example would look like this:

$$NW_n = NW_0 + \sum_{i=1}^{n} [ROI_i(NW_{i-1}) + A_i - L_i]$$

Putting in our forecast for ROI of 0.1 and the $10,000 that their budget says they are able to invest, then we solve for how long it will take to reach their goal when they start with nothing ($NW_0 = 0$).

$$NW_n = 0 + \sum_{i=1}^{n} [0.1(NW_{i-1}) + \$10,000]$$

And we solve for n with $NW_n > \$1,000,000$

We can solve this by using NW + (ROI)NW + A - L over and over again until we have solved the problem. We continue to take what we get from one time period and put it into the next time period until we get to the last time period.

$$NW_1 = NW_0 + (ROI_1)NW_0 + A_1 - L_1 = 0 + \$10,000$$
$$NW_2 = NW_1 + (ROI_2)NW_1 + A_2 - L_2 = \$10,000 + \$1,000$$
$$+ \$10,000 = \$21,000$$

If you do not want to read through all of the steps, feel free to jump ahead to the end of the problem. Each step is really just putting in the number from the previous step and solving the same equation again and then going on to the next step.

$$NW_3 = NW_2 + (ROI_3)NW_2 + A_3 - L_3 = \$21,000 + \$2,100$$
$$+ \$10,000 = \$33,100$$
$$NW_4 = NW_3 + (ROI_4)NW_3 + A_4 - L_4 = \$33,100 + \$3,310$$
$$+ \$10,000 = \$46,410$$
$$NW_5 = NW_4 + (ROI_5)NW_4 + A_5 - L_5 = \$46,410 + \$4,641$$
$$+ \$10,000 = \$61,051$$
$$NW_6 = NW_5 + (ROI_6)NW_5 + A_6 - L_6 = \$61,051 + \$6,105$$
$$+ \$10,000 = \$77,156$$
$$NW_7 = NW_6 + (ROI_7)NW_6 + A_7 - L_7 = \$77,156 + \$7,716$$
$$+ \$10,000 = \$94,872$$
$$NW_8 = NW_7 + (ROI_8)NW_7 + A_8 - L_8 = \$94,872 + \$9,487$$
$$+ \$10,000 = \$114,359$$
$$NW_9 = NW_8 + (ROI_9)NW_8 + A_9 - L_9 = \$114,359 +$$
$$\$11,436 + \$10,000 = \$135,795$$
$$NW_{10} = NW_9 + (ROI_{10})NW_9 + A_{10} - L_{10} = \$135,795 +$$
$$\$13,580 + \$10,000 = \$159,375$$

$NW_{11} = NW_{10} + (ROI_{11})NW_{10} + A_{11} - L_{11} = \$159,375 + \$15,938 + \$10,000 = \$185,313$

$NW_{12} = NW_{11} + (ROI_{12})NW_{11} + A_{12} - L_{12} = \$185,313 + \$18,531 + \$10,000 = \$213,844$

$NW_{13} = NW_{12} + (ROI_{13})NW_{12} + A_{13} - L_{13} = \$213,844 + \$21,384 + \$10,000 = \$245,228$

$NW_{14} = NW_{13} + (ROI_{14})NW_{13} + A_{14} - L_{14} = \$245,228 + \$24,523 + \$10,000 = \$279,751$

$NW_{15} = NW_{14} + (ROI_{15})NW_{14} + A_{15} - L_{15} = \$279,751 + \$27,975 + \$10,000 = \$317,726$

$NW_{16} = NW_{15} + (ROI_{16})NW_{15} + A_{16} - L_{16} = \$317,726 + \$31,773 + \$10,000 = \$359,499$

$NW_{17} = NW_{16} + (ROI_{17})NW_{16} + A_{17} - L_{17} = \$359,499 + \$35,950 + \$10,000 = \$405,449$

$NW_{18} = NW_{17} + (ROI_{18})NW_{17} + A_{18} - L_{18} = \$405,449 + \$40,545 + \$10,000 = \$455,994$

$NW_{19} = NW_{18} + (ROI_{19})NW_{18} + A_{19} - L_{19} = \$455,994 + \$45,599 + \$10,000 = \$511,593$

$NW_{20} = NW_{19} + (ROI_{20})NW_{19} + A_{20} - L_{20} = \$511,593 + \$51,159 + \$10,000 = \$572,752$

$NW_{21} = NW_{20} + (ROI_{21})NW_{20} + A_{21} - L_{21} = \$572,752 + \$57,275 + \$10,000 = \$640,027$

$NW_{22} = NW_{21} + (ROI_{22})NW_{21} + A_{22} - L_{22} = \$640,027 + \$64,003 + \$10,000 = \$714,030$

$NW_{23} = NW_{22} + (ROI_{23})NW_{22} + A_{23} - L_{23} = \$714,030 + \$71,403 + \$10,000 = \$795,433$

$NW_{24} = NW_{23} + (ROI_{24})NW_{23} + A_{24} - L_{24} = \$795,433 + \$79,543 + \$10,000 = \$884,976$

$NW_{25} = NW_{24} + (ROI_{25})NW_{24} + A_{25} - L_{25} = \$884,976 + \$88,498 + \$10,000 = \$983,474$

$$NW_{26} = NW_{25} + (ROI_{26})NW_{25} + A_{26} - L_{26} = \$983{,}474 + \$98{,}347 + \$10{,}000 = \$1{,}091{,}821$$

Notice that their investments would be earning more than they are putting in starting in the ninth year,

$$NW_9 = \$114{,}359 + \$11{,}436 + \$10{,}000 = \$135{,}795.$$

As the years mount up, you really begin to see the effect of time compounding the return on your investments. After twenty-six years, the retirement account is worth more than a million dollars. It may not be easy, but as you can see, it can be done if you stick with it long enough. You may want more than a million dollars to retire, but remember that your retirement account may not be your only asset. For most people their house is their largest asset.

One of the things that you can do with the Equation for Wealth is to figure out what would happen if you made a change to saving or investing. In the example above, you could figure out the result of getting a raise after the first year and saving $1000 of that raise for each year over the remaining 25 years. You can do the math to figure out that you would have an additional $98,347 and your retirement account, after twenty-six years, would then be $1,190,168. You could run as many of these scenarios as you wish and use them to help guild you in making your decisions.

Graphic Example of Investing $50,000 and $10,000 Annually

They say that a picture is worth a thousand words. Graphs can help to picture what a bunch of numbers mean. So I will use a few graphs to help draw a picture of the numbers from a few examples of the Equation for Wealth. The first graph (see Figure 1, "Comparison of $50,000 and $10,000 Annual Investments") compares the couple that invested $50,000 a year to the couple that invested $5,000 a year with the employer matching their investments. Both couples were getting 10 percent annual return on their investments. I will also be using this couple that is investing $10,000 a year for comparison in Figures 2, 3, 4 and 5.

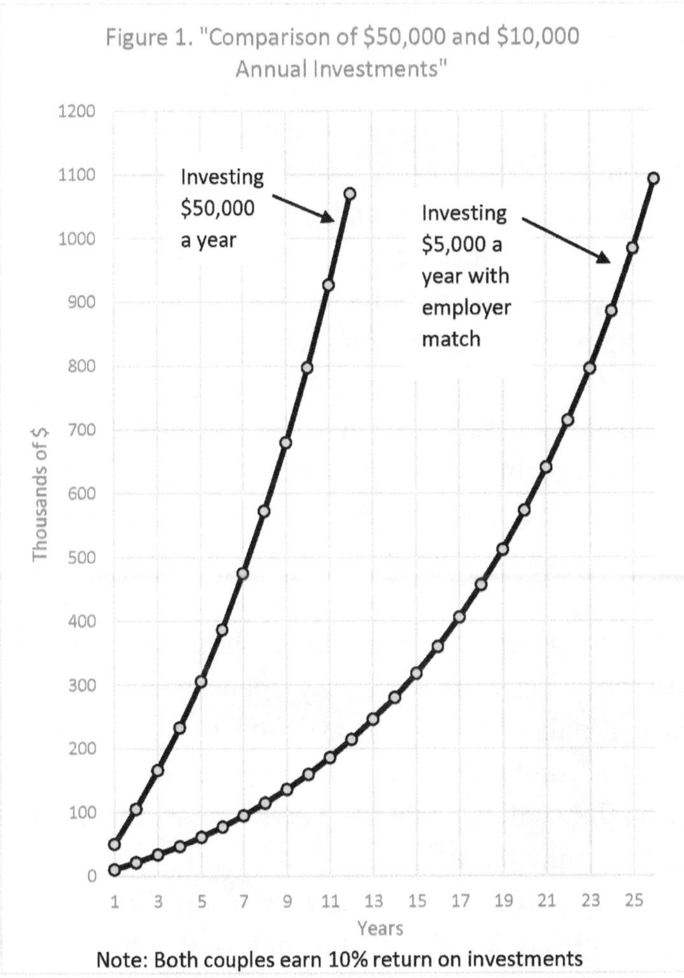

Figure 1. "Comparison of $50,000 and $10,000 Annual Investments"
1200
1100
1000
900
800
700
600
500
400
300
200
100
0
Thousands of $
Investing $50,000 a year
Investing $5,000 a year with employer match
1 3 5 7 9 11 13 15 17 19 21 23 25
Years
Note: Both couples earn 10% return on investments

This graph shows an effect of spending less than you earn and investing the difference. It seems obvious that investing $50,000 a year grows wealth faster than investing $10,000 a year. But investing five times as much does not grow wealth five times as fast. Initially, your wealth will be five times greater if you save and invest $50,000 a year instead of $10,000 a year. As you get some wealth, you will be making money from your investments, and with time the amount of money you are making from your investments keeps growing. As your investments keep growing, the difference between saving and investing $10,000 annually and $50,000 annually becomes less. You will not get rid of the difference, but it will only take you about twice as long instead of five times as long to reach one million dollars investing $10,000 a year as it would if you invest $50,000 a year.

A slight change to the previous example would be to use the budget from a middle-class couple for the difference between what they spend and what they earn, stipulate that they have fifteen years to reach their goal, and then I will calculate what rate of return (ROI) they will need on their investments for them to become millionaires.

They invest $10,000 each year and have fifteen years to become millionaires and again they started with nothing. I have calculated that they would need to get 25 percent annual return on their investments instead of the ten percent that they had been getting in the previous example. Again, by putting in the number that you get for net worth from one step and then putting it into the next, working through the Equation for Wealth for this example would look like this:

$$NW_n = NW_0 + \sum_{i=1}^{n} [ROI_i(NW_{i-1}) + A_i - L_i]$$

Using n = 15 years, and A - L = $10,000

Putting in the $10,000 that their budget says they are able to invest annually and the fifteen years that they have to reach $1,000,000 we then solve for the ROI needed to reach their goal.

$$NW_n = 0 + \sum_{i=1}^{15} [ROI_i(NW_{i-1}) + \$10,000]$$

And we solve for ROI_i

I am hoping that you are getting used to how you know from your budget what the difference is between what you spend and what you earn (A - L). Then you forecast one of two other parameters: either what the return on investment will be (ROI) or what the length of time will be (n) and then you can calculate what the other parameter will need to be to reach your goal. For the rest of the scenarios I would like to stop showing you this difficult looking equation and get straight to solving the problem the easy way.

We will continue to use NW + (ROI)NW + A - L over and over again until we have solved the problem. We will need to put in something for ROI, and we could use trial and error until we get it right, or I can cheat by letting you know that ROI is 0.25. We take what we get from one time period and put it into the next time period until we get to the last time period.

$$NW_1 = NW_0 + (ROI_1)NW_0 + A_1 - L_1 = 0 + \$10{,}000$$

$$NW_2 = NW_1 + (ROI_2)NW_1 + A_2 - L_2 = \$10{,}000 + (0.25)\$10{,}000 + \$10{,}000 = \$10{,}000 + \$2{,}500 + \$10{,}000 = \$22{,}500$$

When you are comfortable with the steps, you can avoid going through all of the iterations and skim to the end to see the answer.

$$NW_3 = NW_2 + (ROI_3)NW_2 + A_3 - L_3 = \$22{,}500 + (0.25)\$22{,}500 + \$10{,}000 = \$22{,}500 + \$5{,}625 + \$10{,}000 = \$38{,}125$$

$$NW_4 = NW_3 + (ROI_4)NW_3 + A_4 - L_4 = \$38{,}125 + (0.25)\$38{,}125 + \$10{,}000 = \$38{,}125 + \$9{,}531 + \$10{,}000 = \$57{,}656$$

$$NW_5 = NW_4 + (ROI_5)NW_4 + A_5 - L_5 = \$57{,}656 + (0.25)\$57{,}656 + \$10{,}000 = \$57{,}656 + \$14{,}414 + \$10{,}000 = \$82{,}070$$

$$NW_6 = NW_5 + (ROI_6)NW_5 + A_6 - L_6 = \$82{,}070 + (0.25)\$82{,}070 + \$10{,}000 = \$82{,}070 + \$20{,}518 + \$10{,}000 = \$112{,}588$$

$$NW_7 = NW_6 + (ROI_7)NW_6 + A_7 - L_7 = \$112{,}588 + (0.25)\$112{,}588 + \$10{,}000 = \$112{,}588 + \$28{,}147 + \$10{,}000 = \$150{,}735$$

$$NW_8 = NW_7 + (ROI_8)NW_7 + A_8 - L_8 = \$150{,}735 +$$

$$(0.25)\$150,735 + \$10,000 = \$150,735 + \$37,684 + \$10,000 = \$198,419$$

$$NW_9 = NW_8 + (ROI_9)NW_8 + A_9 - L_9 = \$198,419 + (0.25)\$198,419 + \$10,000 = \$198,419 + \$49,605 + \$10,000 = \$258,024$$

$$NW_{10} = NW_9 + (ROI_{10})NW_9 + A_{10} - L_{10} = \$258,024 + (0.25)\$258,024 + \$10,000 = \$258,024 + \$64,506 + \$10,000 = \$332,530$$

$$NW_{11} = NW_{10} + (ROI_{11})NW_{10} + A_{11} - L_{11} = \$332,530 + (0.25)\$332,530 + \$10,000 = \$332,530 + \$83,132 + \$10,000 = \$425,662$$

$$NW_{12} = NW_{11} + (ROI_{12})NW_{11} + A_{12} - L_{12} = \$425,662 + (0.25)\$425,662 + \$10,000 = \$425,662 + \$106,416 + \$10,000 = \$542,078$$

$$NW_{13} = NW_{12} + (ROI_{13})NW_{12} + A_{13} - L_{13} = \$542,078 + (0.25)\$542,078 + \$10,000 = \$542,078 + \$135,520 + \$10,000 = \$687,598$$

$$NW_{14} = NW_{13} + (ROI_{14})NW_{13} + A_{14} - L_{14} = \$687,598 + (0.25)\$687,598 + \$10,000 = \$687,598 + \$171,900 + \$10,000 = \$869,498$$

$$NW_{15} = NW_{14} + (ROI_{15})NW_{14} + A_{15} - L_{15} = \$869,498 + (0.25)\$869,498 + \$10,000 = \$869,498 + \$217,374 + \$10,000 = \$1,096,872$$

The next graph (see Figure 2, "Comparison of 25 percent and 10 percent Return on Investment") compares a couple that was able to get 25 percent annual return on their investments to a couple that was getting 10 percent annual return on their investments. In order to reduce the amount of math, I have used the same example as before (Figure 1) for the person that earned 10 percent annual return on their investments. Both couples were investing $10,000 a year.

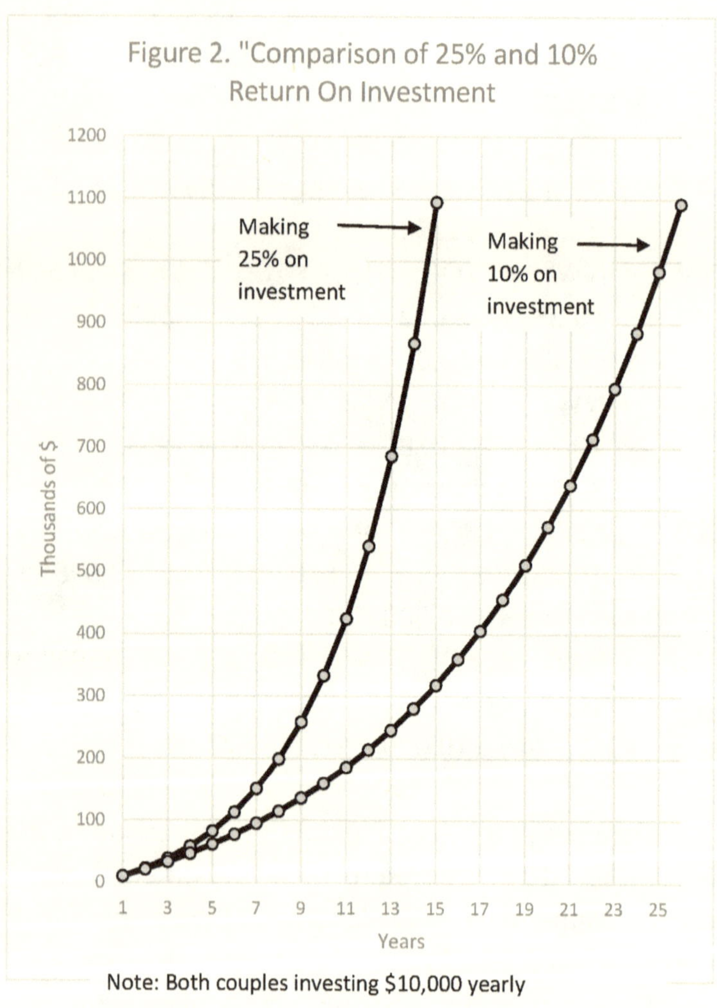

Note: Both couples investing $10,000 yearly

This graph shows an effect of investing wisely. So yes, higher return on your investments does lead to greater wealth, but it also normally leads to greater risk of losing what you invested. Do you think that you can make 25 percent on your investments? And would you be willing to take the risk that corresponds with such a high rate of return?

The wealth that you would get from annual returns on your investments of between 10 percent and 25 percent would be between these two curves. Earlier I said that I would avoid dealing with the math of having the return on investment changing each year. If your rate of return fluctuates from year to year, but always stays between these two curves, then your wealth will also end up to be between these two curves. So if you were investing $10,000 a year in a diversified portfolio with annual returns on your various investments ranging from 10 percent to 25 percent, then your wealth would be between these two curves in Figure 2.

Consequences of Changing Jobs Frequently

What would be the effect if you changed your job after five years and you take the money out of your retirement account (cashing out) instead of putting the money into another retirement account (rolling over) when you leave? You would have to start over again, and you would set yourself back by five years, and therefore, it would take five years longer to reach your goal. What would be the effect if you kept changing jobs and kept cashing out your retirement account? Well, don't expect to have much in your retirement account when you retire.

This next graph (see Figure 3, "Comparing Rolling Over with Cashing Out") compares the couple that invested $5,000 a year with their employers matching their investments to someone who also invested $10,000 annually but changed jobs every five years and cashed out the retirement account each time. In order to reduce the amount of math, I have used the same example as before (Figures 1 and 2). In both these cases, these investors were able to get 10 percent annual return on their investment.

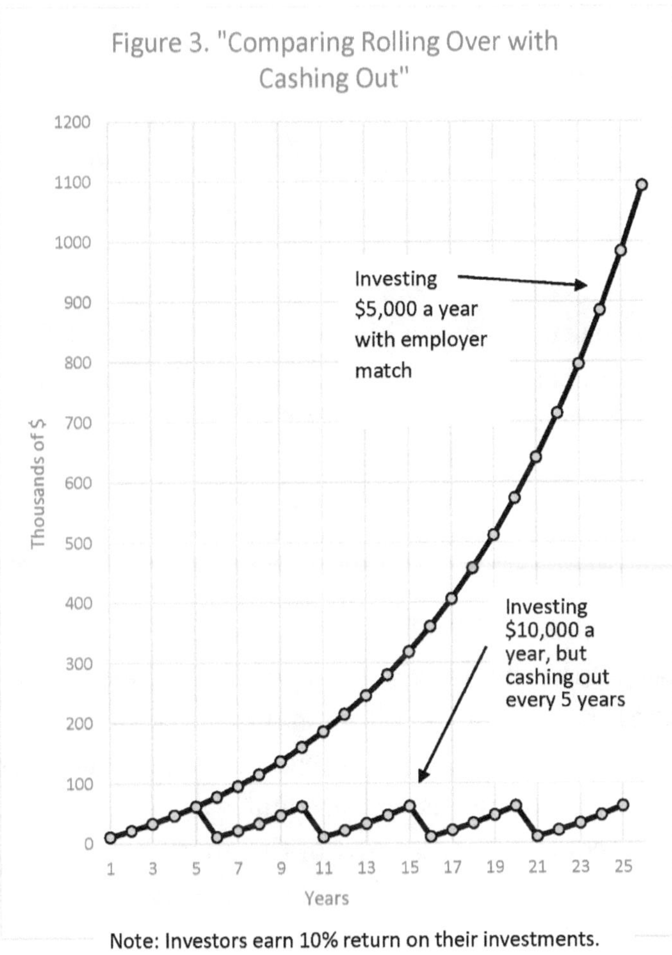

Note: Investors earn 10% return on their investments.

If you keep cashing out your retirement account, you would never have very much money in your retirement account. Taking your money out every five years would have allowed you to spend the $305,255 (five times the $61,051 that is in the account after five years) when you wanted to. If you would have rolled the money into another retirement account when you changed jobs, your retirement account would have more than a million dollars in it. This is a very high price to pay for cashing out your account in order to spend it, and this example did not even include the tax penalty for early withdraw. If you change jobs, roll your retirement fund into another retirement fund, and do not cash it out.

One Consequence of Divorce

One of the reasons a person would cash out their retirement fund is divorce. Bobby's friend, Kyle thought that he was a lady's man, but no one told the ladies. Kyle went to college and majored in partying and getting drunk. He was divorced many times, and each time the retirement account was cashed out so that it could be split as part of the divorce settlement. Not having much money in his retirement account was one of the consequences of his lifestyle.

Taxes

Another factor for your retirement account is

taxes. The government has come up with numerous ways to tax retirement accounts. If I tried to address all of them, I would end up with a book just on taxes. The main concept of taxing investments is either taxing the money before you put it into the retirement account or deferring the taxes until the money is taken out of the retirement account.

In the next example we will invest $10,000 per year taxed at 25 percent so that only $7,500 is actually put into the retirement account each year. Then we will compare this to investing $10,000 a year and taxing it at 25 percent when we take the money out of the account after 26 years. In both cases we will use 10 percent for the annual return on your investment.

Again we solve this by using NW + (ROI)NW + A - L over and over again until we have solved the problem. We take what we get from one time period and put it into the next time period until we get to the last time period.

Net worth in year one equals initial net worth plus return on investments during year one times initial net worth plus year one assets minus year one liabilities.

$$NW_1 = NW_0 + (ROI_1)NW_0 + A_1 - L_1 = 0 + \$7,500.$$

Then repeated for the other years:

$$NW_2 = NW_1 + (ROI_2)NW_1 + A_2 - L_2 = \$7,500 + \$750 + \$7,500 = \$15,750$$

Go through the amount of math that you want. I would suggest you at least go through the way the problem is set up. The setup of the problem can be the hardest part of doing a problem. I have included the math for this scenario.

$$NW_3 = NW_2 + (ROI_3)NW_2 + A_3 - L_3 = \$15{,}750 + \$1{,}575 + \$7{,}500 = \$24{,}825$$

$$NW_4 = NW_3 + (ROI_4)NW_3 + A_4 - L_4 = \$24{,}825 + \$2{,}482 + \$7{,}500 = \$34{,}807$$

$$NW_5 = NW_4 + (ROI_5)NW_4 + A_5 - L_5 = \$34{,}807 + \$3{,}481 + \$7{,}500 = \$45{,}788$$

$$NW_6 = NW_5 + (ROI_6)NW_5 + A_6 - L_6 = \$45{,}788 + \$4{,}579 + \$7{,}500 = \$57{,}867$$

$$NW_7 = NW_6 + (ROI_7)NW_6 + A_7 - L_7 = \$57{,}867 + \$5{,}787 + \$7{,}500 = \$71{,}154$$

$$NW_8 = NW_7 + (ROI_8)NW_7 + A_8 - L_8 = \$71{,}154 + \$7{,}115 + \$7{,}500 = \$85{,}769$$

$$NW_9 = NW_8 + (ROI_9)NW_8 + A_9 - L_9 = \$85{,}769 + \$8{,}577 + \$7{,}500 = \$101{,}846$$

$$NW_{10} = NW_9 + (ROI_{10})NW_9 + A_{10} - L_{10} = \$101{,}846 + \$10{,}185 + \$7{,}500 = \$119{,}531$$

$$NW_{11} = NW_{10} + (ROI_{11})NW_{10} + A_{11} - L_{11} = \$119{,}531 + \$11{,}953 + \$7{,}500 = \$138{,}984$$

$$NW_{12} = NW_{11} + (ROI_{12})NW_{11} + A_{12} - L_{12} = \$138{,}984 + \$13{,}898 + \$7{,}500 = \$160{,}382$$

$$NW_{13} = NW_{12} + (ROI_{13})NW_{12} + A_{13} - L_{13} = \$160{,}382 + \$16{,}038 + \$7{,}500 = \$183{,}920$$

$$NW_{14} = NW_{13} + (ROI_{14})NW_{13} + A_{14} - L_{14} = \$183{,}920 + \$18{,}392 + \$7{,}500 = \$209{,}812$$

$$NW_{15} = NW_{14} + (ROI_{15})NW_{14} + A_{15} - L_{15} = \$209{,}812 + \$20{,}981 + \$7{,}500 = \$238{,}293$$

$$NW_{16} = NW_{15} + (ROI_{16})NW_{15} + A_{16} - L_{16} = \$238{,}293 + \$23{,}829 + \$7{,}500 = \$269{,}622$$

$$NW_{17} = NW_{16} + (ROI_{17})NW_{16} + A_{17} - L_{17} = \$269{,}622 + \$26{,}962 + \$7{,}500 = \$304{,}084$$

$$NW_{18} = NW_{17} + (ROI_{18})NW_{17} + A_{18} - L_{18} = \$304{,}084 + \$30{,}408 + \$7{,}500 = \$341{,}992$$

$$NW_{19} = NW_{18} + (ROI_{19})NW_{18} + A_{19} - L_{19} = \$341{,}992 + \$34{,}199 + \$7{,}500 = \$383{,}691$$

$$NW_{20} = NW_{19} + (ROI_{20})NW_{19} + A_{20} - L_{20} = \$383{,}691 + \$38{,}369 + \$7{,}500 = \$429{,}560$$

$$NW_{21} = NW_{20} + (ROI_{21})NW_{20} + A_{21} - L_{21} = \$429{,}560 + \$42{,}956 + \$7{,}500 = \$480{,}016$$

$$NW_{22} = NW_{21} + (ROI_{22})NW_{21} + A_{22} - L_{22} = \$480{,}016 + \$48{,}002 + \$7{,}500 = \$535{,}518$$

$$NW_{23} = NW_{22} + (ROI_{23})NW_{22} + A_{23} - L_{23} = \$535{,}518 + \$53{,}552 + \$7{,}500 = \$596{,}570$$

$$NW_{24} = NW_{23} + (ROI_{24})NW_{23} + A_{24} - L_{24} = \$596{,}570 + \$59{,}657 + \$7{,}500 = \$663{,}727$$

$$NW_{25} = NW_{24} + (ROI_{25})NW_{24} + A_{25} - L_{25} = \$663{,}727 + \$66{,}373 + \$7{,}500 = \$737{,}600$$

$$NW_{26} = NW_{25} + (ROI_{26})NW_{25} + A_{26} - L_{26} = \$737{,}600 + \$73{,}760 + \$7{,}500 = \$818{,}860$$

The following graph (see Figure 4, "Comparison of 25 percent Tax after and before Withdrawal") compares how the different tax options effect people that invested \$10,000 a year and were getting 10 percent annual return on their investments. One person was taxed at 25 percent when they invested, and the other person was taxed at 25 percent when they withdrew their investments. In order to reduce the amount of math, I have used the same example as before (Figures 1 thru 3) for the person that was taxed when they withdrew their investments.

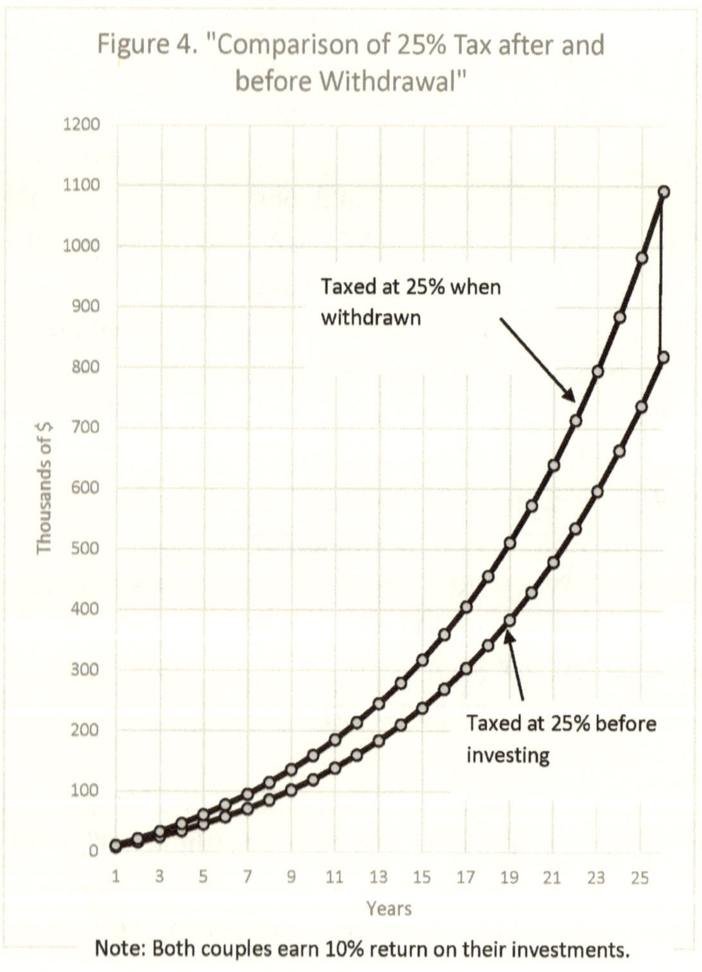

Note: Both couples earn 10% return on their investments.

In this example being taxed at 25 percent before investing resulted in $818,860 after 26 years and being taxed at 25 percent after investing results in $818,866 (0.75 times $1,091,821 of investing $10,000 annually from Figure 1) after 26 years. In both cases the government gets their tax money. Whether you pay them now or later, you can be sure that the government will be collecting taxes. What matters to you is if you are better off paying the government now or later. You may not be able to cheat on your taxes, but you may be able to defer them. You will want to avoid paying taxes on your money before you invest and then also paying capital gain taxes, which is being taxed on the gains from your investments after you invest. Who would want to pay taxes before and after they invest?

Taxes may be more complicated than this example. For one thing you may have different tax rates when you invest and when you sell. This example assumes that you would be in the same tax bracket. You will pay less taxes if you can time it so that you are paying a lower tax rate when you are paying your taxes. When you are retired, you might expect to be in a lower tax bracket. For most of us our income, and therefore our tax rate, will be lower when we retire. If you know that you will have a lower tax rate when you are retired, then it would definitely be wise to have your investments in a tax-deferred retirement account. I am not sure that I trust the government not to raise tax rates. So it might be wise to diversify and have both tax deferred and non-tax-deferred accounts. Diversify the types of your retirement accounts based on what you think your tax rate will be. Most of your retirement accounts should be tax deferred when you think that your tax rate will be lower when you retire.

Consequences of Deferring Saving

When you put off saving and investing for five years, it will take you five additional years to reach your goal of a million dollars than if you didn't put off investing. This should be obvious without going through the math. We will look at how much more you would need to save and invest per year to reach one million at the same time as if you had started saving five years earlier, assuming the first investor is investing $10,000 per year and we are still using 10 percent annual return on investments.

$$NW_6 = NW_5 + (ROI_6)NW_5 + A_6 - L_6 = 0 + \$17,000 = \$17,000$$

$$NW_7 = NW_6 + (ROI_7)NW_6 + A_7 - L_7 = \$17,000 + \$1,700 + \$17,000 = \$35,700$$

Many of you that are tired of the math have already skimmed to the end of the problem. For the others that are tired of the math, what are you waiting for, go ahead and skim to the end of the problem.

$$NW_8 = NW_7 + (ROI_8)NW_7 + A_8 - L_8 = \$35,700 + \$3,570 + \$17,000 = \$56,270$$

$NW_9 = NW_8 + (ROI_9)NW_8 + A_9 - L_9 = \$56{,}270 + \$5{,}627 + \$17{,}000 = \$78{,}897$

$NW_{10} = NW_9 + (ROI_{10})NW_9 + A_{10} - L_{10} = \$78{,}897 + \$7{,}890 + \$17{,}000 = \$103{,}787$

$NW_{11} = NW_{10} + (ROI_{11})NW_{10} + A_{11} - L_{11} = \$103{,}787 + \$10{,}379 + \$17{,}000 = \$131{,}166$

$NW_{12} = NW_{11} + (ROI_{12})NW_{11} + A_{12} - L_{12} = \$131{,}166 + \$13{,}117 + \$17{,}000 = \$161{,}283$

$NW_{13} = NW_{12} + (ROI_{13})NW_{12} + A_{13} - L_{13} = \$161{,}283 + \$16{,}128 + \$17{,}000 = \$194{,}411$

$NW_{14} = NW_{13} + (ROI_{14})NW_{13} + A_{14} - L_{14} = \$194{,}411 + \$19{,}441 + \$17{,}000 = \$230{,}852$

$NW_{15} = NW_{14} + (ROI_{15})NW_{14} + A_{15} - L_{15} = \$230{,}852 + \$23{,}085 + \$17{,}000 = \$270{,}937$

$NW_{16} = NW_{15} + (ROI_{16})NW_{15} + A_{16} - L_{16} = \$270{,}937 + \$27{,}094 + \$17{,}000 = \$315{,}031$

$NW_{17} = NW_{16} + (ROI_{17})NW_{16} + A_{17} - L_{17} = \$315{,}031 + \$31{,}503 + \$17{,}000 = \$363{,}534$

$NW_{18} = NW_{17} + (ROI_{18})NW_{17} + A_{18} - L_{18} = \$363{,}534 + \$36{,}353 + \$17{,}000 = \$416{,}887$

$NW_{19} = NW_{18} + (ROI_{19})NW_{18} + A_{19} - L_{19} = \$416{,}887 + \$41{,}689 + \$17{,}000 = \$475{,}576$

$NW_{20} = NW_{19} + (ROI_{20})NW_{19} + A_{20} - L_{20} = \$475{,}576 + \$47{,}558 + \$17{,}000 = \$540{,}134$

$NW_{21} = NW_{20} + (ROI_{21})NW_{20} + A_{21} - L_{21} = \$540{,}134 + \$54{,}013 + \$17{,}000 = \$611{,}147$

$NW_{22} = NW_{21} + (ROI_{22})NW_{21} + A_{22} - L_{22} = \$611{,}147 + \$61{,}115 + \$17{,}000 = \$689{,}262$

$NW_{23} = NW_{22} + (ROI_{23})NW_{22} + A_{23} - L_{23} = \$689{,}262 + \$68{,}926 + \$17{,}000 = \$775{,}188$

$$NW_{24} = NW_{23} + (ROI_{24})NW_{23} + A_{24} - L_{24} = \$775,188 + \$77,519 + \$17,000 = \$869,707$$

$$NW_{25} = NW_{24} + (ROI_{25})NW_{24} + A_{25} - L_{25} = \$869,707 + \$86,971 + \$17,000 = \$973,678$$

$$NW_{26} = NW_{25} + (ROI_{26})NW_{25} + A_{26} - L_{26} = \$973,678 + \$97,368 + \$17,000 = \$1,088,046$$

This next graph (see Figure 5, "Comparison of $10,000 and $17,000 Annual Investment after 5-Year Gap") compares the couple that invested $5,000 a year with the employer matching their investments to someone that waited five years and then invested $17,000 a year. In order to reduce the amount of math, I have used the same example as before (Figures 1 thru 4) for the person investing $10,000 annually. They were both getting 10 percent annual return on their investment.

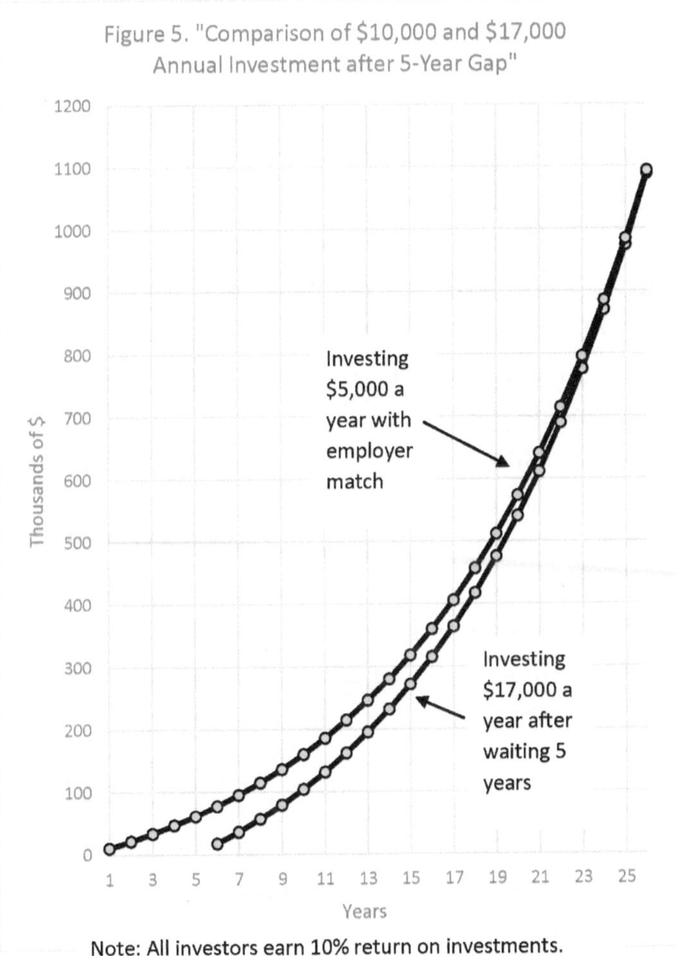

Note: All investors earn 10% return on investments.

This graph shows an effect of investing as long as you can. If you wait to save and invest, then you will need to save a lot more to be able to catch up to the wealth that you could have made. So do not wait, start saving and investing now.

I am only using a retirement account for convenience. Your assets should be diversified, but using one asset reduces the complexity in my examples. You could also use the aggregate of your assets and the average of the return on investment to simplify the Equation for Wealth. If you really wanted to be accurate, you could use each asset with its corresponding return on investment (ROI). I am not sure that it would be worth the effort. Since you cannot really be accurate while estimating what your return on investment (ROI) would be. To be realistic you will not have the same return on investment (ROI) or the same change in assets in each period of time. Putting in different return on investment (ROI), assets (A) and liabilities (L) for each time period will make the equation more realistic but also more complicated. The only time that the Equation for Wealth will truly be accurate is after the time period has passed and you know what the return on investments (ROI), assets (A) and liabilities (L) were, instead of trying to forecast what you think that they might be.

Other Goals

The goals for the previous examples have been

one million dollars, but this goal was used just to allow you to compare the various scenarios. The goals of the previous examples have been geared toward retirement, but the Equation for Wealth will work for other goals and in other situations, as well. The amount of money that you want to obtain represents the goal that you want to achieve, such as retirement, home ownership or whatever you want to achieve.

You get to set your own goals. Once you determine your goal, the Equation for Wealth can tell you what it would take to reach your goal. Then you can determine how you can do what it would take to reach your goal and if it is worth the cost and the risk. You can use the Equation for Wealth for any number of scenarios. If you can think of a combination of spending, earning and investing, then the Equation for Wealth can show you what amount of wealth you will end up with. If your plan does not reach your goal, then you would need to spend less, earn more, invest better or invest for longer.

Home Ownership's Effect on Net Worth

A very common goal is owning your own home. The next scenario will be buying a $200,000 house with a $20,000 down payment. With this scenario you would take out a mortgage of $180,000 and pay down the principle at $12,000 a year for 15 years. You would pay less interest on a 15-year mortgage than on a 30-year mortgage, so I am going to choose a 15-year mortgage. (And it also reduces the amount of math.) You do not pay off the principle of a mortgage at the same rate throughout the life of a mortgage, but to make it simpler I have used one rate for paying off the principle of the mortgage. There are some mortgages that have a penalty for early payoff. For this example, we will use a mortgage without an early payoff penalty, so at any time your only liability is the remaining principle of the loan. The house is initially worth $200,000 and appreciates at 5 percent per year. Getting 5 percent appreciation on real estate would be quite possible and, in many markets, it could be considerably greater.

When you buy a house, there are numerous fees (such as title, realtor, inspector etc.), but you have to pay these at the time you purchase the house so they are not liabilities, and you will not get them back when you sell, so they are not assets either. You will be paying interest on the mortgage, which definitely effects your costs, but it does not affect your wealth. When determining how much house you can afford (how expensive a house you can afford), remember to include all of the costs of home ownership, such as insurance, maintenance and taxes.

Hopefully you have other assets and you do not have other liabilities, but since this scenario is about buying a house, we will only look at the house as your asset and the mortgage as your liability. At the beginning you have the house, which is an asset that is worth $200,000, and you have a mortgage that is a liability of $180,000. So, you have a net worth of $20,000 after buying the house. This is what you had saved for a down payment so you have only exchanged one asset for another, and your wealth has not changed yet.

$$NW_0 = A_0 - L_0 = \$200{,}000 - \$180{,}000 = \$20{,}000$$

Each year the value of the house will go up by 5 percent and the principle on your mortgage will go down by $12,000 (liability decreases by $12,000). Not only do you get an increase of 5 percent of your net worth, you also get the rest of the appreciation of the house, so you get even more assets. The additional asset that you get each year is the return on investment times the principle of the loan that has not been paid off yet. This is called leverage, and you are paying for this leverage with the interest that you are paying on the loan.

So let's put the figures into the Equation for Wealth.

$$NW_1 = NW_0 + (ROI_1)NW_0 + A_1 - L_1 = \$20{,}000 + (0.05)\$20{,}000 + (0.05)\$180{,}000 + \$12{,}000 = \$42{,}000$$

$$NW_2 = NW_1 + (ROI_2)NW_1 + A_2 - L_2 = \$42{,}000 + (0.05)\$42{,}000 + (0.05)(\$180{,}000 - \$12{,}000) + \$12{,}000 = \$44{,}100 + \$8{,}400 + \$12{,}000 = \$64{,}500$$

You are welcome to skim to the end of this problem for the answer when you get tired of looking through the math.

$NW_3 = NW_2 + (ROI_3)NW_2 + A_3 - L_3 = \$64,500 + (0.05)\$64,500 + (0.05)(\$168,000 - \$12,000) + \$12,000 = \$67,725 + \$7,800 + \$12,000 = \$87,525$

$NW_4 = NW_3 + (ROI_4)NW_3 + A_4 - L_4 = \$87,525 + (0.05)87,525 + (0.05)(\$156,000 - \$12,000) + \$12,000 = \$91,901 + \$7,200 + \$12,000 = \$111,101$

$NW_5 = NW_4 + (ROI_5)NW_4 + A_5 - L_5 = \$111,101 + (0.05)\$111,101 + (0.05)(\$144,000 - \$12,000) + \$12,000 = \$116,656 + \$6,600 + \$12,000 = \$135,256$

$NW_6 = NW_5 + (ROI_6)NW_5 + A_6 - L_6 = \$135,256 + (0.05)\$135,256 + (0.05)(\$132,000 - \$12,000) + \$12,000 = \$142,019 + \$6,000 + \$12,000 = \$160,019$

$NW_7 = NW_6 + (ROI_7)NW_6 + A_7 - L_7 = \$160,019 + (0.05)\$160,019 + (0.05)(\$120,000 - \$12,000) + \$12,000 = \$168,020 + \$5,400 + \$12,000 = \$185,420$

$NW_8 = NW_7 + (ROI_8)NW_7 + A_8 - L_8 = \$185,420 + (0.05)\$185,420 + (0.05)(\$108,000 - \$12,000) + \$12,000 = \$194,691 + \$4,800 + \$12,000 = \$211,491$

$NW_9 = NW_8 + (ROI_9)NW_8 + A_9 - L_9 = \$211,491 + (0.05)\$211,491 + (0.05)(\$96,000 - \$12,000) + \$12,000 = \$222,066 + \$4,200 + \$12,000 = \$238,266$

$$NW_{10} = NW_9 + (ROI_{10})NW_9 + A_{10} - L_{10} = \$238{,}266 + (0.05)\$238{,}266 + (0.05)(\$84{,}000 - \$12{,}000) + \$12{,}000 = \$250{,}179 + \$3{,}600 + \$12{,}000 = \$265{,}779$$

$$NW_{11} = NW_{10} + (ROI_{11})NW_{10} + A_{11} - L_{11} = \$265{,}779 + (0.05)\$265{,}779 + (0.05)(\$72{,}000 - \$12{,}000) + \$12{,}000 = \$279{,}068 + \$3{,}000 + \$12{,}000 = \$294{,}068$$

$$NW_{12} = NW_{11} + (ROI_{12})NW_{11} + A_{12} - L_{12} = \$294{,}068 + (0.05)\$294{,}068 + (0.05)(\$60{,}000 - \$12{,}000) + \$12{,}000 = \$308{,}771 + \$2{,}400 + \$12{,}000 = \$323{,}171$$

$$NW_{13} = NW_{12} + (ROI_{13})NW_{12} + A_{13} - L_{13} = \$323{,}171 + (0.05)\$323{,}171 + (0.05)(\$48{,}000 - \$12{,}000) + \$12{,}000 = \$339{,}330 + \$1{,}800 + \$12{,}000 = \$353{,}130$$

$$NW_{14} = NW_{13} + (ROI_{14})NW_{13} + A_{14} - L_{14} = \$353{,}130 + (0.05)\$353{,}130 + (0.05)(\$36{,}000 - \$12{,}000) + \$12{,}000 = \$370{,}786 + \$1{,}200 + \$12{,}000 = \$383{,}986$$

$$NW_{15} = NW_{14} + (ROI_{15})NW_{14} + A_{15} - L_{15} = \$383{,}986 + (0.05)\$383{,}986 + (0.05)(\$24{,}000 - \$12{,}000) + \$12{,}000 = \$403{,}185 + \$600 + \$12{,}000 = \$415{,}785$$

The example of buying a house can be confusing, but it can be simplified because after the mortgage is paid, the effect on your wealth is the value of the house. Fifteen years after buying this house, the house would contribute \$415,785 to your wealth.

This is an example of what leverage can do for you

when the associated asset is increasing in value. Leverage is using debt to purchase assets. Leverage can be very good for you when buying a house, as long as the value of the house goes up. I would not want you to think that leverage always turns out as well as it does when you buy a house. When the associated asset decreases in value, then using leverage will increase your losses. Leverage increases your gain *and* your loss, so you need to be aware of the increased risk if you use leverage. Buying stocks on margin is another example of using leverage, but if your stock goes down even a little, you can lose a lot.

We could also do the math on what the effect of renting would be on your wealth after fifteen years, but sometimes you don't need to do the math to get the answer. You don't really need to have done all of this math to compare buying a house to renting. After you pay off your mortgage, the value of your house is part of your wealth. After years of renting, you still don't own what you were renting, so it does not contribute to your wealth. If you are moving every couple of years, you can be better off renting vs buying because of the costs of buying and selling housing and because you are paying off more of the interest (the money the bank charges you for giving you the home loan) than the principle (the amount of the home loan) at the beginning of your mortgage.

Car Ownership's Impact on Net Worth

Another example could be buying a new car or buying a used car and determining the effect on your wealth after three years. We will not need to use much math for this example. One person buys a new car for $30,000, and the car depreciates by $10,000 over three years. This person's return on investment was the loss of $10,000 over three years. Another person buys a used car for $20,000, and the car depreciates by $5,000 over three years. This person's return on investment was the loss of $5,000 over three years. After three years the first person has $20,000 in wealth from their car and the second person has $15,000 in wealth from their car. The person that bought the new car ends up with a more valuable car, but it depreciated more and they paid $10,000 more for it. If you would have taken the difference that you were paying between the two cars and put it in the bank, then the person that bought the used car would have ended up with more wealth. It is not always just what you did with your money; it is also what you could have done with your money. If you would have taken the $10,000 saved by getting the used car instead of the new car and placed it into an account earning a 10 percent yearly return on investment, then after 25 years, you would have more than $100,000 in the account.

You can make choices that do not improve your wealth. The Equation for Wealth shows you the cost of your decision and allows you to make informed choices.

It is your choice if you really want to buy that new car. You can look at what you want to do and the Equation for Wealth will tell you the effect on your wealth. The Equation for Wealth will not make decisions for you, but it will show you what the consequences will be and allow you to make informed decisions.

Negative Net Worth From Debt

So far most of the examples have been of how your wealth can grow. Sometimes the choices that we make do not turn out as well. If you are spending $1,000 more than you earn each year and putting the debt on credit cards that have 20 percent yearly interest, what would happen to your wealth after 10 years if you started with no net worth? This is spending more than you earn and investing the difference poorly by using high interest credit card debt. You may be able to guess that this will not turn out well.

Let's put the figures into the Equation for Wealth.

$$NW_1 = NW_0 + (ROI_1)NW_0 + A_1 - L_1 = 0 - \$1,000$$

The net worth after the first year would be -$1000.
Since you end up with $1,000 in liabilities, your net worth is negative.

After the second year, the net worth is -$2,200.

$NW_2 = NW_1 + (ROI_2)NW_1 + A_2 - L_2$ or $NW_2 = -\$1,000 + (0.2)(-\$1,000) - \$1,000 = -\$1,000 - \$200 - \$1,000 = -\$2,200$.

Notice that everything is negative, since what you have are all liabilities.

The math is included for the other years. When you want, you can skim to the end of the problem to see the answer.

$NW_3 = NW_2 + (ROI_3)NW_2 + A_3 - L_3 = -\$2,200 + (0.2)(-\$2,200) - \$1,000 = -\$2,200 - \$440 - \$1,000 = -\$3,640$

$NW_4 = NW_3 + (ROI_4)NW_3 + A_4 - L_4 = -\$3,640 + (0.2)(-\$3,640) - \$1,000 = -\$3,640 - \$728 - \$1,000 = -\$5,368$

$NW_5 = NW_4 + (ROI_5)NW_4 + A_5 - L_5 = -\$5,368 + (0.2)(-\$5,368) - \$1,000 = -\$5,368 - \$1,074 - \$1,000 = -\$7,442$

$NW_6 = NW_5 + (ROI_6)NW_5 + A_6 - L_6 = -\$7,442 + (0.2)(-\$7,442) - \$1,000 = -\$7,442 - \$1,488 - \$1,000 = -\$9,930$

$NW_7 = NW_6 + (ROI_7)NW_6 + A_7 - L_7 = -\$9,930 + (0.2)(-\$9,930) - \$1,000 = -\$9,930 - \$1,986 - \$1,000 = -\$12,916$

$$NW_8 = NW_7 + (ROI_8)NW_7 + A_8 - L_8 = -\$12{,}916 + (0.2)$$
$$(-\$12{,}916) - \$1{,}000 = -\$12{,}916 - \$2{,}583 - \$1{,}000$$
$$= -\$16{,}499$$

$$NW_9 = NW_8 + (ROI_9)NW_8 + A_9 - L_9 = -\$16{,}499 + (0.2)$$
$$(-\$16{,}499) - \$1{,}000 = -\$16{,}499 - \$3{,}300 - \$1{,}000$$
$$= -\$20{,}799$$

$$NW_{10} = NW_9 + (ROI_{10})NW_9 + A_{10} - L_{10} = -\$20{,}799 +$$
$$(0.2)(-\$20{,}799) - \$1{,}000 = -\$20{,}799 - \$4{,}160 -$$
$$\$1{,}000 = -\$25{,}959$$

Notice that it only took five years for the interest on your debt to exceed what you were adding to your debt by overspending. Just as your debt can grow, your debt can also spiral out of control. Time is on your side when you were growing your wealth, but time is working against you when you are growing your debt. The way to stop your debt from spiraling out of control is to start spending less than you earn and use the difference to pay off your debt. The longer you take to change direction and get your spending under control, the greater the debt that you will have to pay off.

Our fictitious friend Alex loved gadgets and always had to get the latest ones. Alex had a good paying job as an engineer but was spending too much and racking up credit card debt. Alex took out a home equity loan to pay off the credit card debt, but kept spending too much and ended up with both credit card debt and a loan to pay off. On the positive side, Alex had an automatic payroll deduction to get the maximum employer contribution, but he found himself tempted to take funds from the retirement account to pay off the credit cards. He knew that was costly, and he realized he had to make some lifestyle changes. He just didn't know how. Alex had a hard time not giving in to the impulse of buying every new gadget that he saw. Alex also had trouble with patience, and waiting to pay off debts before making new purchases was very difficult for him. He felt he would never get out of debt unless something changed. He did some studying and learned how to slow down his impulse spending by making a simple budget with an allowance for gadgets. He learned to ask himself questions before making a purchase and taking at least a day to look for bargains. He considered if he really needed to buy it or if he just wanted to and if it was the right time to buy it. He kept asking himself these questions until it became a habit, and he became reasonably successful at spending more wisely.

The Equation for Wealth can be used to see the effect on your wealth from individual choices like investing in a retirement account, buying a house or buying a car. When you combine all of these individual choices together, the Equation for Wealth will give you the total effect on your wealth. It is your choice as to how much you want to look at whether you are trying to make a decision on one thing or you are trying to keep track of all your investments. When it has to do with the accumulation of wealth, you can use the Equation for Wealth. You can do the math for as many of your scenarios as you wish. If you really do not want to do the math at all, then remember my Formula for Wealth: spend less than you earn and invest the difference wisely for as long as you can.

For those that would like more examples of using the Equation for Wealth, you can work through these next couple of examples. If you start with $100,000 and earn $25,000 more than you spend each year, and your goal is $1,000,000 in four years, then the Equation for Wealth can tell you what your rate of return on your investments would need to be. It is quite another thing if you are comfortable with that amount of risk and the real chance of going broke. If you don't want to do the math, the answer is that you need a rate of return of approximately 75 percent. You have very little chance of actually accomplishing 75 percent return on your investment. The Equation for Wealth can tell you what it would take to get the outcome that you are looking for, but that does not necessarily mean that you will be able to do what would be required to get there.

$$NW_1 = NW_0 + (ROI_1)NW_0 + A_1 - L_1 = \$100{,}000 + (0.75)\$100{,}000 + \$25{,}000 = \$200{,}000$$

$$NW_2 = NW_1 + (ROI_2)NW_1 + A_2 - L_2 = \$200{,}000 + (0.75)\$200{,}000 + \$25{,}000 = \$375{,}000$$

$$NW_3 = NW_2 + (ROI_3)NW_2 + A_3 - L_3 = \$375{,}000 + (0.75)\$375{,}000 + \$25{,}000 = \$681{,}250$$

$$NW_4 = NW_3 + (ROI_4)NW_3 + A_4 - L_4 = \$681{,}250 + (0.75)\$681{,}250 + \$25{,}000 = \$1{,}217{,}188$$

If you are only comfortable with the risk associated with a rate of return on your investments (ROI) of 5 percent and you again start with $100,000 and can save and invest $25,000 yearly, then the Equation for Wealth can tell you how many years it will take to reach one million dollars. (If you do not want to do the math, the answer is 20 years.)

If you want to come up with a couple of scenarios of your own, you should be able to churn through the numbers. You can use your budget to determine the difference between what you earn and what you spend and then use that for assets minus liabilities (A - L). If you have a safe portfolio, then 5 percent would be a reasonable return on your investments (ROI), and if it is a risky portfolio, then 10 percent or even 15 percent would be reasonable.

If you want to do a lot of these scenarios, then I would suggest that you use a computer because it will get very tedious. If my investment with this book goes well, then I may be able to create a website with a computer program to calculate the Equation for Wealth for you. If you really cannot wait for my website to have this program, then you can try one of the retirement calculators that are out there. There are plenty of retirement calculators available on the internet, but many of them are used as advertisement. If you use one of the retirement calculators, be careful that it is not designed just to sell you an investment product.

Accuracy of the Mathematical Equation

So how accurate is the Equation for Wealth? The Equation for Wealth will be as accurate as the information that you supply it. When you use wildly optimistic forecasts of your income, expenses and rate of return on your investments, then you will get a wildly optimistic projection of what your wealth will be. If you budget for saving $6,000 a year and you do not keep to your budget, then the calculations that you made based on saving $6,000 a year will not come true. The calculations that you made would then tell you what could have been if you had kept to your budget. When your forecast of your return on your investments is inaccurate, then the calculation based on your forecast will also be inaccurate. The calculation would show you what would have happened if you had been able to meet your forecast for the return on your investments.

We are normally optimist in our forecasts. Don't feel bad if your forecasts are off by a little or even a lot. There are people that get paid to make these kinds of forecasts, and they are really not that accurate either. Does it really matter to you how precise the projection is, or is it the direction of the projection that matters? Is it important that the equation gives the correct projection within 5 percent accuracy or that it projects the correct direction for you? In addition to making projections of what your net worth will be, you should also be determining what your net worth actually did become, and then you will know how well you did at making forecasts.

How What We Have Discussed Fits Into the Equation

All of the parts of the Equation for Wealth have already been discussed in the previous parts of this book. You can see where each section of the principles that we have discussed fits into the equation.

$$NW_n = NW_0 + \sum_{i=1}^{n} [ROI_i(NW_{i-1}) + A_i - L_i]$$

Assets minus liabilities (A - L) is spending less than you earn and involves budgeting. Return on investment times net worth [(ROI)NW] is investing wisely, which involves risk tolerance, diversification and asset allocation. The summation is to invest wisely for as long as you can and is the effect of time.

Dealing with assets minus liabilities or spending less than you earn, is often referred to as personnel finance. Personal finance could be looked at as how you get some wealth now by spending less than you earn so that your assets are greater than your liabilities.

Dealing with return on investment times net worth or investing wisely, is often referred to as wealth management. Wealth management could be looked at as how you grow the wealth that you currently have by investing wisely so that you will have even more assets in the future. It takes dealing with both personnel finance and wealth management to grow wealth, but you need to start with your personal finances if you are going to get any wealth to manage.

The Equation for Wealth is an equation that can be used to project what your wealth could be. Whether you like the answer to an equation does not change what the answer to the equation is. The only way to change the answer to an equation is to change what you put into the equation. So, how do you make the best of it? The decisions that are in your control are the decisions that could make your life better based on what decisions you make. There are really only a few factors in the Formula for Wealth that you can control, how much do you spend, how much do you earn and how you invest what you have. The Equation for Wealth will show you what will happen when you change one of the factors in the Equation for Wealth. The Equation for Wealth can show what changes to make, but it is up to you to make the changes to get what you want. To improve the answer from the Equation for Wealth you need to spend less, earn more, invest better or invest for longer. If you were to make poor choices and spend more than you earn or invest poorly, then the Equation for Wealth would tell you how much poorer you would become.

If you were looking for a get rich scheme, then I am sorry that I have disappointed you. The Formula for Wealth is not a get rich scheme or a scheme of any kind. Math can be used to describe the nature of things and the Equation for Wealth can be used to describe the nature of wealth. The Equation for Wealth does not cause wealth, but it does describe the way that wealth is built. To increase your wealth, increase your assets, decrease your liabilities and make as much as you can from the assets that you have. Just getting the number is not the same as understanding the principles that go into that number. Even if you dislike math, there are things that can be learned from the Equation for Wealth without going through the math. You gain wealth when you acquire assets, reduce liabilities and maximize the rate of return on your assets. If anything does not affect these, then it will not affect your wealth. The bigger the difference between how much you make and how much you spend, the greater your wealth. The greater the return on your investments and the longer they have to grow, the greater your wealth. This really is all there is to the Formula for Wealth. Sounds rather simple when stated this way, so why isn't everyone wealthy?

Chapter 6

If It's Simple,
Why Isn't Everyone Wealthy?

Factors that affect your ability to apply
the Equation for Wealth to your life.

Math can be used to describe what is. Having an equation for the effect of gravity on rockets does not change gravity, but it does allow us to make better rockets. Having an Equation for Wealth does not in itself change wealth, but it does allow us to make better decisions with our wealth. It is not rocket science; you can use what you learn from the Equation for Wealth to help you reach your goals. You will still need to properly apply what you learn from the Equation for Wealth.

When you are not reaching your goal, then all you need to do is to spend less or earn more or invest better or for longer. When your goal is to be as wealthy as you can be, then spend as little as you can, earn as much as you can and get the highest return on your investments that you can for the level of risk that is acceptable to you and invest for as long as you can. Being simple and straight forward does not mean it is easy. If it was easy, then everyone would be wealthy. Spending less than you earn and investing wisely for as long as you can sounds simple, but you still have to do it. Hard work and determination will be needed to build your wealth. It takes self-control to spend less than you earn. It takes planning to invest wisely, and it takes patience to invest wisely for as long as you can.

You could come up with a budget that has a difference between what you spend and what you earn that allows you to invest $10,000 a year, and you could expect to get 10 percent yearly return on your investments, so the Equation for Wealth would tell you that you will become a millionaire in 26 years. This does not mean that you will become a millionaire. You still need to stick to your budget, and you need to make 10 percent yearly return on your investments. The Equation for Wealth will tell you what it will take, but until you do what it takes to meet your projections, the Equation for Wealth is telling you *what could be.*

So, you have seen that there is an equation that tells you what you need to do to grow your wealth. Does this mean that you are going to do what it takes to increase your wealth? People do not behave like equations. Many people have problems following through with their plans. Sometimes we will not do what we should, even when we know what we should do. Often, we do what we want to do instead of what we know we should do. Do you want to hear what the Equation for Wealth is telling you or will you be in denial so that you can continue to spend as much as you want? Seeing that there is an Equation for Wealth might help you to be more rational about your own wealth. Even if you choose not to do what you know you should do, the Equation for Wealth will show you what it would cost you if you don't do what you know you should do.

Revisiting Our Fictious Friends

There are emotions that make it harder to spend less than you earn. Kyle had trouble controlling his lusts and desires. He kept getting married and then divorced. Kyle had a problem with drugs and alcohol. He was an alcoholic and had a hard time changing his life style. He went into rehab but had a relapse and continued to struggle to stay sober. Keith was an angry and violent man. He had no control of his emotions, and he suffered from bouts of rage. Those around Keith also suffered from his rage. Keith had gotten into bar fights and one time seriously hurt someone. He was not planning to go to jail; he was just lashing out. When he got out of jail, his criminal record made it hard for him to get a job.

Rowan had never had to work because he was fortunate to come from a wealthy family, but that left him unfocused, undisciplined and he had had trouble finishing what he started. His rich parents spoiled him and did him no favors. Bobby and Erin were immature when they got married, but grew to be persistent and self-controlled once they learned to work together. Erin had problems with recklessness, and Bobby had issues with being overly cautious, but they adjusted to each other and learned to work well together.

We all have different personalities, and some personality traits make it more difficult to spend less than you earn. Your personality traits will affect what investing wisely is for you. We all have strengths and weaknesses. How we deal with them can make a lot of difference. Knowing yourself can help you to know what traits you need to work on and what investment styles you are best suited for.

Instant Gratification

There is nothing in the Formula for Wealth about feelings, but your feelings can get in the way of building wealth. When you feel that you are entitled to everything, then you will spend all of your money and end up broke. Unless your parents are very rich, you will not find anyone that will buy you everything that you think you are entitled to. When you feel like you deserve a new car or you feel like you just have to have a new dress or expensive shoes, then you will have trouble controlling your spending. You may need to start by controlling your feelings to be able to control your spending. When you have trouble controlling your spending, you are likely to spend more than you earn and your wealth will decrease. Feeling like you need to keep up with your friends when your friends have debt that they cannot keep up with, will just leave you with debt that you cannot keep up with, either.

There are a lot of people that have trouble spending less than they earn. It can be difficult to be content with what you have. If you can be content to live within your means today, then you can have more for tomorrow. Living for today and spending what you have now will ensure that you don't have any savings for tomorrow. Spending money as fast as it comes in and spending all of the money that you get is a sure way to ensure that you are not building wealth. Self-control or will power will be required to avoid the snare of instant gratification. Starting to control your spending can be the hardest part, so just start living within a budget and see what happens. Controlling your spending and keeping a budget should get easier the more that you do it.

Your ability to avoid instant gratification will go a long way toward building wealth. In order to invest wisely, you need to save something to invest. In order to save, you need to resist the urge to spend all that you have as soon as you get it. Do you want to spend your money today or do you want to have even more money to spend later? When you spend your money today, it does not have a chance to grow and become even greater wealth.

Market Pressure

One of the problems that we have with spending less then we earn is that a lot of people want us to spend more. They want us to buy their products, and they are good at advertising their products. You need to stay focused on your goal so that you can avoid buying that new product that they are advertising or that deal that they are trying to talk you into. There is always someone that wants to separate you from your money, and they keep coming up with new ways to get you to spend your money. The next time that they want you to spend money on what you don't really need, think of what else you could do with your money.

Our culture not only makes it hard to stay on a budget, but after you have spent too much, there are lots of people that want to loan you money. There are home equity loans, which make sure that you don't build equity in your home. It seems like every store has a credit card that they want you to use. Just because the culture makes it hard to stay within your budget, does not mean that it is not worth doing. Sometimes it is worth being different than other people, especially when they are broke and in debt.

Credit Cards

As I mentioned when I was talking about budgeting, one of the mistakes that we make is allowing the use of credit cards to cause you to lose control of your spending. Spending cash or using a credit card is still spending. The more that you are separated from your payment, the harder it is to control your spending. Credit cards can make you feel separated from what you are spending and can lead to overspending. Those that are trying to sell you something, do not want you to be thinking about what it will cost you. When you are unaware of what you are paying while you are spending, then it's easy to lose control of your spending. If you cannot pay off your credit card balance at the end of the month, then you may be spending too much on your credit cards, and it may be time to think of getting rid of your credit cards.

You could avoid revolving credit cards by using companies that arrange loans with prearranged installments. No matter how you borrow money, you are still spending more than you earn. To grow wealth you must do the opposite and spend less than you earn. A better way to avoid credit cards is to use prepaid debt cards or use cash.

Automatic Payments

Another way to be separated from your payment is by having payments automatically deducted from your account. Automatic deductions are convenient, but they can make controlling your spending and budgeting more difficult. If automatic deductions effect your ability to control your spending, then the convenience is not worth the cost.

Not all automatic deductions are bad. Automatic

payments into a savings account can get you started saving something so that you can begin investing. Automatic contributions to a retirement account can separate you from the temptation to spend all of your money now instead of preparing for your future.

Children

I would not say that kids are a bad investment. In fact, they may be the best thing to invest your life in. But having children can make it hard to keep spending under control. Not only do you have the extra cost of feeding and clothing a child, but it can also be hard to say no to a child that wants a new toy or the latest gadget. How do you explain how much will be sacrificed in the future if the child gets that new toy today (opportunity costs)? Some adults have trouble understanding or accepting opportunity costs, and it can be so much harder to get a child to understand. Older children should be taught the basics of money management. Children see what they want now and may not understand that it means not being able to get something else later. How do you explain to a child that if you get them all of the toys that they want, there will not be any money left to buy the things that they need? It can be very hard for a parent to tell a child that they cannot have everything that they want when they want it. You may not have to say no to your grandkids if you make the right choices when you are a parent.

Fear

It is a mistake to let fear cause you to sell investments after the market has already gone down and you end up selling low. Do not invest based on what has already happened, invest based on what you think will happen. You want to buy low and sell high, but just avoiding buying high and selling low would help. In the short term the market goes up and down. It is best to ignore the short-term swings in the market. Otherwise all that you are likely to do is to make a lot of transactions and make your broker wealthy off your transaction fees. It would be better to have a diversified portfolio and then not get worried about the daily swings in the market. Look at what your investments do over a longer period of time (years).

Do the Best That You Can

Life is not fair. It is easier for the rich to get richer. The rich can get richer, but the poor do not have to get poorer. The Equation for Wealth does not say that the poor have to get poorer. In fact, it says that anyone can get richer. Starting out poor does not mean that you have to stay poor. An unfortunate thing about wealth is that when you are poor, it is harder to build wealth, and when you are rich, it is easier to build wealth. When you are poor, you may be spending all of your income on necessities, so that you do not have anything left to invest and grow into wealth. The Equation for Wealth does not address how hard it is to come up with the money to make investments, but it gives you directions and lets you know what can be done. You could complain about how someone else has it easier, or you could focus on what you can do for yourself. What really matters is how you get richer, which is to increase your assets, decrease your liabilities and invest wisely to get a good return from the assets that you have.

No matter how long or difficult the journey is, it consists of steps and starts with the first step. Even if the journey is short, you will not get anywhere if you don't take the first step. The first step in the journey toward wealth is to spend less than you earn by decreasing your spending and increasing your income. The second step is to invest wisely by understanding your risk tolerance, paying off debt and diversifying by having multiple types of investments. The third step is to invest wisely for as long as you can. Since you cannot start any sooner than now, this means starting to spend less than you earn now and starting to invest the difference wisely now. The best time to start the journey toward wealth is now, so that you are able to invest wisely for as long as you can.

So, what has happened to Bobby, Erin and friends?

Bobby was able to retire, but chose to postpone retirement and worked a few more years in order to be able to help the kids get settled as adults. Bobby and Erin wanted to be able to give the kids the help that their parents were not able to give them. Erin is a couple of years younger than Bobby, so having Bobby wait a couple of years to retire also allowed Bobby and Erin to retire at the same time.

At their retirement party, Bobby and Erin caught up with some of their old friends. Alex had paid off his credit card debt and was working at paying off his home loan. Alex had a retirement account and thought that he might be able to retire in a few more years. He had some design ideas for a new gadget and couldn't wait for the extra time that retirement would give him. Blair and Frankie did quite well financially. Being a doctor and a lawyer, they had two very good incomes and found a financial advisor that they could trust to manage their finances the way that they wanted. They invested in low-cost mutual funds and exchange-traded funds. Blair and Frankie made millions and became as wealthy as Rowan's family. Rowan, after one class in business, thought that he could conquer the business world and invested in trendy stocks but always seemed to get into the latest hot stock as others were moving on to the next hot stock, so he missed the boat more often than not. Rowan had also joined his fellow businessmen in investing in high rise apartment buildings, but unfortunately, he did not make as much as expected because the supply usually exceeded the demand. Rowan fell back on family money time and time again, but fortunately there was enough buffer in the family fortune to cover his half-hearted and often failed attempts at investing.

Many of their old friends did not save and invest and wondered how they could afford to retire. These friends could not see how they would make ends meet on Social Security and did not feel financially secure. A couple of Bobby's friends blamed their ex-spouses and the alimony payments for not being able to invest anything. Kyle's drinking led to several divorces as well as tickets for impaired driving. He was fired a few times due to his alcoholism and often moved between towns. What little money he had was spent on drinking. Kyle lived in poverty. Keith, the high school bully, had been arrested several times over the years for fighting and eventually ended up in prison. No one saw him after that.

After their retirement party, Bobby and Erin decided to sell their house. They packed up and moved near one of their children so they could be close to their grandkids. During their retirement they took a few of the trips that they had always wanted to take. They also had plenty of time to spend with their grandkids. They enjoyed their retirement to the fullest.

Chapter 7

Other Tips for Success

Productivity

Productivity is related to income and therefore wealth. Generally, the more that you produce, the more income you will earn. But what you produce needs to be worth something. Producing a little of what is worth a lot, is as valuable as producing a lot of what is worth a little. Producing a lot of what is worth a lot should give you a very nice income. Being productive is not enough to guarantee that you will become wealthy. Being unproductive almost certainly guarantees that you will not become wealthy. Do not expect to get rich while you are in your parent's basement playing video games. When you are not being productive, you are still consuming, either what you saved, what the family had saved or what you can get from others, such as taxpayers.

Hard Work and Persistence

Being lazy is a good way to avoid wealth, but hard work alone will not build wealth. When you make lots of money and spend lots of money, you do not end up accumulating wealth. I am not one that believes that with hard work everyone could become millionaires. If everyone was a millionaire, then a million dollars would not be worth all that much. I do believe that with hard work and wisdom, everyone can do better for themselves.

Get rich schemes and short cuts do not normally work out. Often you end up worse off. Ponzi schemes (funds paid by later investors that are used to pay artificially high returns to the original investors) are one example. The first investors have a high rate of return on their investment, so they get rich if they don't get caught and go to jail. Most Ponzi scheme investors will have a negative rate of return on their investment and lose what they had. When it sounds too good to be true, the odds are that it is too good to be true. You may want to get rich quick, but that is not how it normally works. Most of us have to save and invest a little at a time and for longer than we might wish. Very few have such a large income that they can get rich quickly. What you can do is to work toward getting rich, which will help you can get rich as quickly as possible.

Persistence can pay off. Getting rich takes time since very few win the lottery and get rich overnight. It normally takes many years to build significant wealth.

The Good and the Bad of Investing in Education

The return on investing in education can be very good if it results in a good paying career, or it can be negative if you end up with student debt and do not get better employment than if you never went to college. Rate of return from education depends on marketability of the degree, how long will you use the degree and also what happens if you don't finish the courses needed to get the degree. One student can learn a trade skill and make a good living while another takes out student loans to go to college but does not find a good job and ends up broke. It is possible to end up getting a negative return on your investment in education.

If you drop out before finishing and you took out loans to go to school, you will be worse off than if you did not go to college. Studying something that you have no aptitude for can lead to failure. Not being serious about your education can also lead to failure. Very few are able to party all night and then do well in class the next day. Dropping out of school costs you time and money, both of which you could have used more wisely.

If everyone studies for the same occupation, then there will not be enough jobs in that occupation for all of the students. If too many students study law, then there is no more need for lawyers. Yes, I know that is a fantasy, but it helps to illustrate a point. If there are already too many in your occupation, then you can branch out to find another occupation. When there are too many lawyers, some of them can then become politicians.

Studying for an occupation that you hate could lead to a miserable life. You need to decide if choosing an occupation that you dislike is worth whatever extra money you might earn doing the job. There is nothing wrong with learning to make buggy whips, if that is what you want to do. But if you are studying something for which there are not any jobs, then what you are really studying is a hobby. You need to find something between a hobby that is enjoyable but doesn't pay and an occupation that pays well and makes you miserable.

Let's look at some examples, using our fictitious friends. Bobby and Erin invested in their education to improve their employment status after they were settled into married life. Alex graduated from engineering college and got a good paying job that eventually helped to pay off the student debt. Blair went to nursing school and also worked in the medical field while studying to save up funds for graduate school. Blair still needed to borrow a good deal of money to finish medical school, but not as much as most other medical students. Kyle went to his chosen party college and excelled at that, but did not gain any useful skills. After a couple of years, he dropped out without finishing a degree. Unfortunately, he built up student debt without getting any real education. Adding this financial pressure to his other lifestyle woes meant he was still paying off student debt very late in life.

Rowan studied whatever subject sounded good at the time. Rowan was lucky to have rich parents and avoid student debt, but Rowan's lack of common sense led to him not having a useful education, either.

Pay Off Debts

Paying off your debt is a wise investment. Normally, it is the wisest investment that you can make. If you are in debt, then I would advise that a large portion of what you can invest goes toward paying off your debt. Paying off debt is like investing in yourself. Instead of buying bonds, which is someone else's debt, you are buying back your own debt. As I've said, where else can you find a low risk investment with a return as high as the interest that you are paying on your debt? And paying off your debt is very low risk. Investing in paying off your own debt is as close as you will get to a risk-free investment.

Pay off your credit cards every month. If the balance is more than you can pay off, then you are spending beyond your means. Which means it is time to reduce your spending or it is time to get rid of your credit cards. When you get a lump sum of money, such as tax return or inheritance, it would be wise to use it to help pay off your debt.

Getting a consolidation loan to reduce the interest on the debt you already have may sound nice, but too often it leads to taking on more debt. If you get a consolidation loan, it would be a good idea to look at the fees on the loan. Then you really need to determine whether you will be able to start living within your means so you can pay off the consolidation loan. Do not get a consolidation loan unless you take care of the underlining problem of spending too much. Otherwise you will end up adding more credit card debt in addition to the consolidation loan. Unless you take care of the underlining problem of spending more than you earn, you will only be digging yourself into more and more debt. Whether it is a personal loan or credit card debt, it does not really change much, it is still a liability. The interest rate may change a little bit, but remember that the lowest interest rate you can get on debt is to not have any debt.

I would not recommend a reverse mortgage or any other type of loan. Loans are not a good way to build wealth. Sometimes you need a loan. Depending on your needs and alternatives, a reverse mortgage could be a good choice. It is best to avoid payday loans if you can because they have very high interest rates. It is normally best not to borrow at all, but if you have to borrow, then do your homework and get the lowest interest rate that you can. Pay off your debt as soon as you can, and set aside some liquid assets (such as cash, savings, etcetera) so that your next problem does not force you to go back into debt.

The people lending you money make more money when they can get you to borrow more. So, of course, they are going to encourage you to borrow as much as they can. The day that you become free of debt is the day you stop helping others grow wealth and start to grow your own wealth.

When you borrow money, you should ask if you will get as much for the money as it is going to cost you. Will the rate of return that you get on the borrowed money be greater than the interest rate that you have to pay on the loan? Most of the time the answer will be no. The only way that your net worth increases by borrowing money is if you are able to make a greater return on the money than what borrowing the money costs you.

Corporate debt is often used because of tax advantages, and you may be tempted to think that debt will help reduce your taxes. You could end up spending more than what you could save on your taxes. In case there is any question about it, in general, debt is not a good way to grow wealth; it is normally a good way to grow poorer.

Help from Debt Councilors

Spending a little bit of money for assistance in developing your plan for getting out of debt will be worth it if it makes the difference in getting you started paying off your debt and helps you to keep at it. Don't give hundreds of dollars to someone to help you pay off your debt. Instead, put that money toward your debt, spend less and pay down your debt even more.

Financial Advisors

Before you have much money, a financial advisor is not likely to make more money for you than what they will charge you. Until you have some wealth, a financial advisor would not be worth the cost. You should have enough wealth so that the value of the advice is greater than the cost of the advisor. There is some free advice on the internet. Free advice may be worth what you paid for it and is often advertising for what someone wants to sell you. They may be trying to sell you an investment product so that they can make commissions. Multiple companies offer low-cost index funds that would not require a financial advisor. If you go with one of the larger companies, you should be able to avoid making mistakes while you begin investing. After you have accumulated some investments, you can see if a financial advisor would be right for you.

If a financial advisor does not know enough about you to give you good advice, they may only be trying to sell you their investment product. Your wealth is very personal. How much are you able to earn? How little can you spend? How much wealth do you have to begin with? How much investment risk are you comfortable with? How long can you keep building and growing your wealth? The answers to these questions and many more will help an advisor determine what investment plan would be wise for you. Make sure your advisor asks you these types of questions.

Many financial advisors like to advertise that they

are "fiduciary" and will give advice based on your best interests. In the United States all financial advisors could say this since there are regulations intended to ensure that financial advisors act in their client's interests. Regulations do not change human nature. The advisor may still act in their own best interests whenever they can. You should question if the financial advice is unbiased or if the advisor is trying to sell you something. You could look into fee only advice in an attempt to avoid advisors that are trying to make a commission by selling you their investment product. Of course, you would want to find advisors that charge low fees. Do not get a false sense of security, it is still up to you to look out for your own interests. You need to learn enough about investing so that you know when someone is just trying to sell you their investment product or worse yet when someone is trying to scam you out of your money.

Ultimately it is your choice whether you'll follow the advice of a financial advisor, but if you are not going to listen to the advice, then why pay someone for the advice? Be careful how much you pay for advice. You could easily pay more for advice than the advice is worth to you. You should not pay financial advisors more than the extra amount that they can earn for you on your investments. Even good advice is not worth more than the amount that you can earn by using the advice.

Perhaps the best reason for a financial advisor is to get advice that is not tainted by your emotions.

Emotional financial decisions are usually wrong. Not wanting to listen to the voice of reason will not change what reason is trying to tell you. Wanting something to be true will not change what reality is. When you make financial choices based on what you want to be reality, you will often be making the wrong choice. Before you make financial decisions, start by determining what your real choices are.

By now you know that I recommend investing wisely, but there are many ways to invest wisely. When someone recommends a particular stock, fund or other investment product, then I often wonder what is in it for them. Is what they are recommending going to give them the largest commission for selling you that investment product?

Trading Too Much

The cost of trading has come down, but it still costs money to make trades. If you are trading frequently, then you may not be earning enough to cover your cost of trading. Even if you earn enough to cover the cost of trading, the cost of frequent trading will still reduce the return on your investment. If you really enjoy the thrill of trading, at least remember to subtract the cost of trading when you are determining your return on your investment, so that you know what you are really making on your investments.

Understand What You're Investing In

Whether you are buying or investing, make sure that you know all of the costs. When you buy a car, they like to add on extra costs to the price of the car. When you invest, they may also like to add on costs to what you are paying for your investment.

Do not invest in things that you do not understand. When you do not know about what you want to invest in, then do some research and learn more about the investment. Learn enough to avoid making a mistake, but that could be hard since even the experts make mistakes. You may have to settle for learning enough to avoid making a lot of mistakes. You do not need to be a genius with your investments to invest wisely. To invest wisely all you really need to do is to avoid making mistakes. Of course, the better that you invest, the greater your wealth will grow.

Greed

Sure, you could do better if you make 15 percent return on your investment then if you make 10 percent return on your investment. Taking too much risk in order to get higher returns on your investment can be a mistake. What can be too risky for me may not be good enough for you, but greed can be a mistake that prevents you from making money or may even cause you to lose what you invested. Being greedy can lead to trouble and cause you to lose a lot of money when you make very risky investments.

Having a good income is important, but what you do with your income is just as important. Working an extra job or two will increase your income. Is it worth it to wear yourself out trying to get richer or would it be wise to show restraint with spending and be satisfied with less? We can all do more to make more money, but we may not want to do what it takes to make more money. It comes down to whether you want the extra money enough to do what it would take to earn it. The Equation for Wealth can tell you what it will take to become rich but not if it is worth what it will take to become rich. It can be hard to know what is enough and be wise enough to be content when you are ahead.

Being Frugal

I have discussed multiple times that spending less than you make so that you can spend the difference on buying assets or paying off debt, is the beginning of growing wealth. One way to reduce your spending is to not buy things that you don't need. Do you really need to spend money buying fancy coffee every day? Being frugal would include not buying unnecessary things, like the latest cellphone when the one that you have is still perfectly usable. Do you really need the latest gadget or that fancy new car?

When spending money, ask yourself: Do I need it? Can I get it cheaper? and Is now the right time to buy it? Whether you need it comes down to two things: can I make do with what I have; and before you pay someone to do something, could you do it just as well yourself? Doing some research online to see if you can get it cheaper has become easy. What you need to determine is Can you find it on sale? Can you find a coupon? Is it cheaper in bulk? Would you be able to buy it used? and Is there a generic or store brand that costs less? Whether now is the right time to buy depends on how long you can keep using what you have before it wears out and whether there is a better time to buy, such as waiting for a close-out sale.

Just taking a moment to question if you really want to spend money will help you to control your spending. It will also help you to think about how much you are spending. People that are trying to sell you their product do not really want you to think; they would prefer that you buy without realizing how much you were spending, that you don't look for a better deal somewhere else or think about if you really need to buy right at this moment.

Personally, I like to focus on value. Value is getting a low price relative to the value of what you buy. This does not mean that you get the cheapest or the most expensive. Buying the cheapest may mean that it doesn't last and it turns out to be a poor value. Buying the most expensive may mean spending extra for quality that you don't need or buying because of the brand name. Value means that you get the most that you can for the money that you spend. Buy at the lowest price that you can while getting the quality that you need. Don't pay for top quality when you don't need top quality, and you rarely need top quality. Get the level of quality that you need, and don't overspend for what you don't need.

If you are not going to use it, then don't buy it, even if it is a good deal. If you don't use it, it will not be a good value for you. When you don't make good use of something, then it cannot be a good value to you. If you buy a new car and it just sits in the garage, then it will not be a good value to you, even if it is a good car. To get good value from a car, you need to drive it, and the more miles that you can drive it, the better its value to you. So, you should not get a replacement car until you have driven the one that you have for a while.

One way to have money is to not spend what you have or more importantly do not waste what you have. Thriftiness could really just come down to not wasting your money. It is your decision on how thrifty you will become before you become miserly. Generally, the common problem is spending too much, not being miserly.

Being Too Frugal?

Being frugal or even cheap is a good way to spend less than you earn. When does being cheap adversely affect the life that you could have lived and cause more regrets than the regrets caused by being a little poorer? No one else can know how much you value wealth. Do you want to live in a shack now for a chance to live in a mansion later? You have to make the choice, and you will be the one to live with the consequences of your choice. It is your choice, no one else can make it for you.

Renting and Leasing

Avoid renting or leasing whenever possible. When you rent or lease, you are buying the right to use something, but you do not own it, so it costs you money without increasing your assets. What you are doing is paying to borrow it for a period of time. However, if you buy something, then your assets increase by the value of what you bought. There are a couple of times when renting is sensible. It is sensible to rent when you cannot afford to buy, such as renting an apartment while you build up a down payment to purchase a house. It is also sensible to rent when you only want to use the item for a short period of time, such as renting tools or renting an apartment when you expect to be moving.

Instant Gratification and Impulse Control

Plan your shopping trips so that you know what you are planning to buy, and then only buy what you were planning on buying. You should not need to go shopping all of the time. Plan your shopping trips so you can consolidate trips. This will help cut down on gas and avoid excessive shopping. Waiting to buy something until you can shop around to find a good deal will not only help you avoid being stuck with a bad deal, it will also help to avoid impulse purchases. Taking the time to investigate an offer to make sure that it is not a scam will not only help you avoid impulse purchases, it will also help you avoid being conned. Many mistakes are made because of not taking the time to think things through, so take the time that you need to make a good decision.

If you don't spend your money now, then you will have more money to spend later. When you spend your money today, it does not have a chance to grow and become greater wealth tomorrow. It is your choice how and when you spend your money. The choice should be a conscience choice, instead of spending money without knowing either how much you spend or what you spent it on. Instant gratification does not build wealth. When you spend your income, or even worse go into debt to buy what you want now, then your money will not be growing to build wealth. When you borrow to spend today, you will owe even more money tomorrow. You will end up with growing liabilities and have even less wealth tomorrow.

Employer Matching Contribution

If your employer offers to match part of your contribution to a retirement fund, then do what you can to get the maximum amount of matching funds. It is just like free money, so take all that you can get. When your employer matches your contribution to a retirement account, you are doubling your investment. Where else would you be able to get 100 percent return on your investment. When an employer gives you a benefit like matching your contribution to a retirement account, then not taking advantage of this benefit is like not taking the pay check for the wages that you have earned.

Avoid Owning Stock in the Company You Work For

Try to avoid only owning the stock of the company that you work for. That is the opposite of diversification. If the company goes bankrupt, not only do you lose your job, but your stock has lost its value at a time when you need the money from that stock. If your company gives you their stock or stock option, then take what is free or at a good price, but you may want to sell most of it so that you can buy other stocks to diversify.

Conventional Wisdom

Most people in the United States can avoid poverty by finishing high school, getting any job, not having kids out of wedlock and not being a criminal. For more on this you could see Ron Haskins "Three Simple Rules Poor Teens Should Follow to Join the Middle Class" or other similar work. It would be better if after finishing high school you then go on to college or vocational school. Raising kids is worth it but it is not easy, it is expensive and it is harder if you are doing it alone. You are not going to get rich on government handouts. If you get married, stay married, because divorce can be very costly. It may be worth the cost of divorce when you are in a bad marriage but it will be expensive. Along with the emotional pain and the many other problems caused by divorce, divorce is also expensive. Anytime that you get lawyers involved it gets expensive. Excessive alcohol use or drug use can cost a lot more than the cost of the drugs and alcohol. There is also DUI, divorce, getting fired and what you could have done if you had been sober. You should do all right when you get married before having children, stay married, get an education for gainful employment, work hard, avoid idleness, avoid substance abuse and avoid crime.

Do what you can to be healthy because, among other things, being sick can be expensive. Even if insurance pays your health care bills, it will not pay you back for what you could have done while you were sick. Being healthy may be beyond your control, but there are some things that you can do, such as exercise and eating right.

You may be thinking that a lot of this stuff is the same thing that your parents and others have been telling you. There is a reason for conventional wisdom. Conventional wisdom is what has worked for most people most of the time. This does not mean that conventional wisdom will work best for you in every situation. You may think that you know better than conventional wisdom, but be careful if you stray too far from conventional wisdom. The Equation for Wealth can show you how and why conventional wisdom has worked. Whether or not conventional wisdom works in your situation, the Equation for Wealth can show you the financial outcome for your situation.

Social Security and Medicare

The government tends to complicate whatever they do, and Social Security and Medicare are no exception. Social Security and Medicare are complicated partly because of government regulations and also because the right decision is different for different situations. There are a few basic truths, but beyond these you will need to research what is best for your individual situation.

The best time to claim Social Security is when you need it, but if you do not need it right away, then how long you wait to claim Social Security depends on how long you will live. If you are in poor health, then you will probably be better off starting to take your Social Security benefits as soon as you can. If you are in good health, then you will probably be better off waiting until you are 70 before starting to take your Social Security benefits. If you are married, remember to consider how it will affect your spouse when you are determining when to take Social Security benefits.

Everyone that is eligible should sign up for Medicare Part A as soon as they can. Signing up for the other parts of Medicare depends on what health insurance you already have. Study your Medicare options ahead of time, and make your choice within three months of your 65th birthday. One thing for sure is that lots of people will try to sell you Medicare supplement plans, but what would be right for you depends on what you have and what you may still need. If you are considering Medicare supplement plans, use an agent that represents multiple plans.

Do Not Stay in a Bad Position

When you make mistakes, do what you can to fix your mistakes and then more on. That fishing boat that you tried to convince your wife was an investment may be an asset but only for the amount that you can sell it for, which is not what you bought it for. You are only likely to lose money on it, so stop trying to convince your wife that it was a good investment. Try not to make your financial situation worse by putting more money into a bad decision. Sometimes the best that you can do is to cut your losses by getting out of a bad choice before you make it worse. When you do not like your situation, then you have to do something different in order to change your situation. Doing the same thing and expecting a different outcome has been referred to as insanity. Even if you are not crazy, trying to get a different outcome by doing the same thing will lead to failure.

Apply the Principles to Your Life

I like how the Equation for Wealth shows the truth behind what we have been told we should do. What really matters is *what you do*. Applying the principles of the Equation for Wealth to your life is the Formula for Wealth.

Summary

It is normal to call this portion of a book the conclusion. That makes me think that this is the end. We may have come to the end of this book, but now you get to start implementing the concepts of this book. You can use the Equation for Wealth to project what will happen to your wealth. If you stay with a budget and forecast either your return on investments or how long you will invest, you can then calculate how much wealth you will have. You could also use the Formula for Wealth if you do not want to go through the math. Start spending less than you earn and investing the difference wisely for as long as you can (the Formula for Wealth). The greater your income, the less your spending, the wiser your investments and the longer you invest, the greater your wealth will be.

How much wealth you will have after a period of time is pretty simple to describe. It is how much wealth you started with plus how much that grew during that period of time plus how much more wealth you made during the period of time. The Equation for Wealth is your initial net worth plus the rate of return on your initial net worth plus how much you added to your initial net worth and this is repeated over multiple time periods. Using a day as the increment of time, then the Equation for Wealth says that the wealth you'll have tomorrow is the wealth you had yesterday plus how much it grew today plus the wealth you acquire today.

The Equation for Wealth is not the most important part of this book. What is more important is that you understand what it means, how it applies to you and that you start applying it to your financial situation. Knowing that there is math behind what you have been told and therefore much of what you were told was true, should help to motivate you to do what you know you should be doing. There are things that can be learned from the Equation for Wealth without going through the math. How do you acquire assets, eliminate liabilities and maximize the return on your assets? The bigger the difference between how much you make and how much you spend, the greater your wealth.

The first of the factors in the Formula for Wealth that you can control is to spend less than you earn so that you can use the difference to buy assets or pay off debt. You either have to increase your income or decrease your spending. It is not just your income that matters for building wealth, it is the assets that you acquire with your income. This means that you cannot spend all of your income on other things and expect to still buy assets to build your wealth.

Controlling your spending starts with knowing what you are spending and knowing what you are spending starts with a budget. Without some form of a budget you have no idea what you are spending your money on. At the end of the month you could end up broke and have no idea where the money went. Your budget is what you plan on spending; you then need to execute your plan.

Just earning more than you spend is not enough to ensure wealth if the assets you acquire lose their value. The second factor in the Formula for Wealth that you can control is to invest wisely. There is nothing that you can do now about what your current net worth is, but there are things that you can do about what your net worth will be. There are things that effect the return on your investments that you cannot control. You can protect yourself by diversification and do the best that you can to forecast what would be wise investments. You are not likely to find an investment that is better than paying off your own debt.

You need to have some money available to take care of the problems that come up so that you can deal with the problems before they become a crisis that you cannot deal with. If all of your income is going to making payments, then you are only one problem away from a crisis. You need some money available for unexpected problems, and how much depends on how much you are willing to risk not being able to deal with problems that come up.

How much is your piece of mind worth to you, and how much risk is right for you? You need to choose the general level of risk that is acceptable to you. Generally, when you have high returns, you will have high risk, and when you have low risk, you will have low returns. The best that you can do is to get the highest return possible at a level of risk that is acceptable to you. Determine the level of risk that you are comfortable with and then strive for the highest return at that level of risk.

You cannot avoid mistakes, but being diversified will avoid a mistake turning into a disaster. Diversity would be having multiple types of investments (such as cash, gold, property, stocks and bonds). Don't put all of your money into one investment or even one type of investment.

The idea of mixing risky and safe investments is quite common. The goal is to get a better return at an acceptable risk. Investors will often do this by putting some money in risky stocks in hopes of high returns and some of their funds in safer blue chips stocks or bonds. One common way is to mix 60% stocks with 40% bonds. There are numerous options on what is the best mix to maximize the rate of return on your investments while keeping the risk manageable. The common distribution of assets is a good place to start, and if you deviate very much, you should make sure that you understand why.

The third of the factors in the Formula for Wealth that you can have a little control over is time. There is not a lot that you can do about time. There is not much that you can do about the mistakes of the past except to learn from them. All that you can do is to make the most of the time that you have by starting to spend less than you earn and investing the difference wisely.

Wealth is personal. While it may be personal, it

involves some of the same things for all of us. What are your goals? How much can you earn? How little can you spend? How wisely can you invest? and How long can you invest? What I believe is wise investing for anyone is 1) to ensure that you get the most from any matching contribution to your retirement account from your employer 2) pay off your debt 3) have some liquid assets and 4) invest in a diversified portfolio.

So why isn't everyone as wealthy as they could be? Either people do not understand what it takes to build wealth or they do not do what they know will build wealth. Now that you have read this book, you should have a good understanding of what it takes to build wealth. Does this mean that you will become a millionaire? It is possible that knowing the Formula for Wealth will not make you wealthier; it will depend on what you do with that knowledge. I hope that I have provided you with sound practical advice. No matter how good advice is, it is not of any use until you make use of it. It is your choice how you make use of the information and advice that you have. It is now up to you to do what you know will build wealth.

I wish you success in applying the Formula for Wealth to your life by spending less than you earn and a long life of investing the difference wisely. I hope that you get a lot of what you want and all of what you need.

Appendix

Applying the Equation for Wealth Beyond Individuals

There is more to wealth than personal wealth. Having a general idea of what makes up the wealth of a company may help you in determining which companies are worth investing in. Having a general idea of the wealth of countries may help you to know what countries you would like to live in or to go to when looking for work. Understanding how the Equation for Wealth is applied to companies and countries can be interesting, even if you do not use that information to affect your personal wealth.

Companies

Just like for individuals a company's and a country's net worth tomorrow is its net worth today plus the return on its net worth, plus its change in assets minus its change in liabilities: $NW_1 = NW_0 + (ROI_1) NW_0 + A_1 - L_1$. What makes up these terms and what changes them is not the same for individuals, companies and countries. Changing the meaning of terms, changing goals and changing motives can have a large impact on applying the Equation for Wealth to companies and countries. Companies and countries also have more difficulty putting a monetary value on the terms that go into their Equation for Wealth. In addition, a country has more things to consider than monetary wealth.

Valuing assets for a company is not as easy as valuing deposits, stocks and bonds. Companies have equipment that could be valued for what it could be sold for, referred to as liquidation value. Liquidation value is not normally used until the company goes bankrupt. What matters is what the company can produce. Corporate value could be thought of as their profits or more precisely the present value of their future profits. Profits could be looked at as being similar to a person's income. Although profits are sales minus expenses, it is only somewhat similar to income minus expenses.

The value of a company is often looked at from one of two views. Either the company is going under or it is continuing to do business. If it is going under, then the value of the company is what you can sell its assets for. If the company is staying in business, then its value is the net present value of the cash flow from the company. This is a fancy way of saying its value is its future income and return on that income. At any given time, you only care about one of these, but they both apply. If you combine these two ways of looking at a company's value, you have the current net worth plus the sum of future profits and the rate of return on those profits. This is really then just another way of saying the Equation for Wealth using corporate terms.

For public companies the stock market could be used to determine its value. For an investor a company is worth what they can get for its stock. The company's stock should be worth the present value of the future cash flow from the company. This would be the present value of dividends and the present value of the stock when they sell the stock. This may sound like a definition of corporate worth, so does that mean the stock price should be used to determine the value of a company? You could say that a company is worth whatever its stock is worth in the stock market. The stock price is a convenient method to determine the value of a company, but you sacrifice accuracy for convince. Does the worth of a company really go up and down with the stock market? Do we have a better idea of the value of a company? Not really. Like anything else a company is worth what you can get for it. When a company is put up for sale, you will find out what it is really worth. Until then the stock price is a reasonable indication of what you can get for the company, and it also has the advantage that it is easily observed and measured.

Putting a value on intangibles related to the company (such as brand name, reputation, data, staff knowledge, customer satisfaction, innovation, etcetera) can be very difficult. How can a company value its intangible assets? Is it really anything other than an educated guess? What is the value of customer

170

loyalty and how would you measure it? How do you value goodwill? What is the value of passing a family company to the next generation and the value of controlling a private company?

There are costs that a company creates but does not have to pay for. The fancy term for this is called externalities, and an example is environmental damage caused by the company. Are these part of the company's liabilities? How does this factor into the value of a company or does it affect the value of a company? When all you have are educated guesses, then use what you think is the best guess that you have, but it is still just an educated guess.

Figuring out the net worth of a company can be difficult. Luckily, it does not matter very much what method you use as long as you are consistent about which method you use and you accept the lack of accuracy. Any method will allow you to track trends, so that you can see what direction the company's net worth is going and approximately how rapidly. If a company does something to improve productivity but their net worth goes down, then you should think about changing course because something other than productivity may be the real issue.

To apply the Equation for Wealth to a company, forecast return on investment, assets and liabilities and then calculate net worth. This is very similar to applying it to individuals except that it is more complicated. It is still assets, liabilities, return on investments and time, but what these terms entail and how they are obtained are different for companies than for individuals. Starting with the Equation for Wealth and making some simplifying assumptions works well for individuals, but this does not work well for companies. Most individuals acquire assets from the difference between what they earn and what they spend. So we were able to assume that the difference between assets and liabilities is approximately the same as the difference between earning and spending, but this assumption is not very accurate for companies.

What are the assets and liabilities of a company, and how are they acquired? Assets of a company are not as clear cut as personal assets. A lot of corporate assets are determined by earnings minus expenses, but companies produce assets, and when they produce more than they sell, they become inventory. Corporate assets would also include intellectual capital, like patents and intelligent, adaptive employees. Corporate liabilities are such things as bonds or unfunded pensions and accounts-payable. You have little choice but to do the best that you can at determining what the changes in assets and liabilities are when looking at a company.

Companies hire accountants to keep track of all of their assets and liabilities. Companies and value investors could benefit from a computer program that applies the Equation for Wealth to companies to determine current wealth of companies, projecting the future wealth of companies and help in the decision-making process by determining the effect on the wealth of a company from various choices by projecting the impact on the wealth of a company from business decisions.

Companies have to get equity or bonds, and the tax effects of borrowing can make borrowing a wise choice. When the owner provides the equity, then when they pay off debt, they are betting on their own company. The choice to borrow is not as obvious for companies as it is for individuals.

Increasing the factors of production is an investment in the wealth of a company. The factors of production are equipment, people, ideas, etcetera. Instead of return on investment, companies often refer to return on equity, but the concept is still the same, even if some terms get renamed. Return on equity is how much money you make on the money that you put into your company.

Countries

How do you measure the wealth of a country? Is it what the government has or what the people have? Measuring national assets can be difficult. Do assets for war and destruction count or do only productive assets count? How do we value defense and survival? If weapons are not used, are they worthless or did they buy peace? If investing in military capacity prevents war, then it is a wise investment, but how do you measure it? How do you value allies and enemies? These things exist and they effect nations, so how do we account for them. Ideas can enrich a nation as much as material wealth or production. So how do we place a value on ideas? What is the value of a new computer program? Even harder, how do you value ideas like freedom and property rights?

The normal way to measure the income of a nation is Gross Domestic Product (GDP) or Gross National Product (GNP), depending on whether it is produced within the country's borders or by the people of the nation. Gross Domestic Product has its limitation; it does a poor job of accounting for social value and costs. How does a country value good health care, low pollution, culture, etcetera?

Some of the assets of countries are property, natural resources, infrastructure, companies and people. Countries start out with natural resources, but how do they use them? Some countries have oil reserves that they sell but then squander the wealth on unprofitable programs or ill-conceived projects. Sometimes the wealth is stolen by the leaders and elites. Some countries start out with little but rocks and find it hard to even grow potatoes. Through hard work and innovation, they can still become first world countries.

Neither the assets or liabilities of a country are clear cut. When a country has liabilities, it is uncertain what those liabilities will really turn out to be. One example is pension funds. There may be a promise of a certain amount of pension payments, but when it comes time to pay out the pensions, they may only pay a portion of what was promised. What a government will do in the future is uncertain, and there is very little that can really be done to force them to keep their promises. Current liabilities may be known, but what really are the liabilities that the country will fulfill in the future.

Public debt problems can cause everyone to feel the pain of the financial problems. How much can a country afford to borrow before everyone feels the pain of a bankrupt and failed country? The cost of debt changes between counties and also with the times. Even if you know the current safe level of debt, conditions change. When times are safe, interest rates are lower and debt more manageable. When times become dangerous, then interest rates rise and debt can become unmanageable. There was a time when economists would agree that government debt above 100 percent of GDP was a tipping point that would cause sustained slowdown of the economy. Now that many governments have high levels of debt, there is debate over what level of debt reduces economic growth, and there are also many countries experiencing slow economic growth. It is debatable when the tipping point is that government debt will have an impact on the general public. We can agree that when a government cannot finance their debt, then the country is already in trouble. There have been many nations that have been crushed by debt, and there will be many more, but when the next one will be crushed by debt is hard to forecast.

Countries become richer by steadily becoming

more productive over a long period of time. But how do countries become more productive? Do countries become rich due only to capital accumulation? Then why would we care about the quality and quantity of labor? The factors of production are equipment, people, ideas, etcetera. The productivity of labor provided by the population of a country is a major component of the productivity of the nation. Do countries become rich due only to applying new methods and technology to produce more from the capital and labor that they have? There are political characteristics required for countries to become rich, like taxes, stability, the rule of law and property rights. There are social and cultural factors that affect the productivity of countries such as institutions, families, independence and ambition. It is all of these factors that help countries to become more productive. All of these factors affect the Equation for Wealth of a country.

Productivity has been improved through industrialization, leading to a few rich countries. There is a vast difference between developed countries and poor countries. The real increase in Gross National Product per person only started in the 18th century with the Industrial Revolution and did not affect all countries equally. Many poor countries lack the stable growth-oriented government needed to build an industrial base. War and unrest can be very hard on productivity because it kills workers and destroys factories and other means of production. When the oppression, corruption or inequality grows too great, the people revolt. This reduces wealth during the chaos and violence of a revolution and its aftermath. Unfortunately, the new government is often no better than the one that it replaced.

The productivity of the population is a large factor in a nation's wealth, so should you use productivity as a large factor in determining who is allowed to immigrate into a country? Immigration is not all bad or all good. It depends on who is allowed to immigrate into the country. Allowing criminals to enter a country is not likely to end well. We should be able to determine who most of the criminals are and then try to keep them out. Getting the energetic, talented and educated to come to your country will add to Gross National Product growth and therefore increase the country's wealth. Immigration benefits a country as long as the country chooses who immigrates based on merit and the immigrants can be absorbed in a controlled manner.

Basic economics students know the principles of supply and demand. Sometimes supply is too great and prices drop. Sometimes demand is high and prices rise. In American politics, supply-side economics is associated with the right and is also called trickle-down economics. Demand-side economics is associated with the left and is also referred to as Keynesian economics. Politicians seem to have a solution and are looking for a problem to justify implementing their solution. Instead of looking for the solution to the problem that we have, both right and left want to apply their solution no matter what the problem is. When demand is high and prices are rising fast, the left would still favor demand-side economics by increasing government spending. When supply is great and prices are dropping, the right would still favor supply-side economics by reducing regulations on business. For politicians, implementing their solution and agenda can be more important than solving the problem.

Is there production capacity that is going unused and needs an increase in demand to make use of the excessive capacity? When there are barriers to investment and production, then there may need to be an increase in supply. When there is need of greater supply, is the problem excessive regulation, graft, excessive taxes or even confiscation of the assets of production? Could the problem be that inflation is so high that no one expects a real return on their investments? Could debt be so high that there is nothing left to invest to increase production? Is government spending being wasted? It is normally best to start by determining what the problem is before determining how to fix the problem. All too often governments start with what solution they want to use instead of what policies fix the existing problem and make the nation wealthier.

Maximizing wealth is not all that matters and should not be the only goal. The compounding effect of time on the Equation for Wealth helps to ensure that the rich get richer. When government policy assists the concentration of wealth in a few elites, the country may be wealthier while most of the population is poorer. Concentrating wealth in a few monopolies may improve productivity and increase the nation's wealth while making most of the citizens worse off. When government policy reduces productivity while evenly spreading the wealth, then you will have less than the maximum wealth that the country could have. It is nice to have more wealth to spread around, but it also matters how the wealth is distributed. So, we have a continuing debate on how to grow wealth and on how the wealth should be distributed, which means plenty of employment for lawyers and politicians.

Property rights and the rule of law are what governments need to provide to allow individuals to prosper. When there isn't the rule of law, then the factors in your Equation for Wealth can be changed at any time by someone else. For wealth creation, I would say that the most important thing for a government to provide is stable property rights. It is hard to build wealth in a country that does not have property rights. When you do not have a right to own property, then whatever wealth you build up will be taken from you. If you do not own it, then after you go through the work of improving it, someone else will take it and benefit from your work. Why would you build up a business that you know someone will take from you? Just about everyone is wise enough to figure out that it is not worth the effort, when someone else benefits from your efforts. People will work only as hard as they must and will avoid working for the benefit of others whenever they can get away with it.

What country you live in can have a major impact on your wealth. If a country is poorly run, it can have a major impact on the wealth of its citizens. The leaders could steal the wealth of the nation or follow poor policies. What can you do other than try to leave for better opportunities? Customers can leave companies that do not deliver a good product. Some of the population can leave a country that does not deliver a decent life, unfortunately not everyone may be able to escape.

The Equation for Wealth is applicable to companies and countries. Applying the equation to increase wealth for companies and counties can lead to greater wealth for individuals. Here is hoping that corporations and politicians apply the Equation for Wealth in a fair and equitable manner.

Glossary

Annuities: Annuities are contracts, created by insurance companies, that provide a predicable future income by providing payments of a fixed sum of money at regular intervals of time. There are a large variety of annuities, but they are normally for the annuitant's lifetime and are designed per insurance company mortality tables. Often the annuity is bought with a single payment based on the annuitant's age when they will start receiving payments. The younger the annuitant is when they start receiving payments, the greater the cost of the annuity. The cost of annuities increases when interest rates are lower.

Assets: An asset is something desirable and valuable. Assets may be either tangible (cash, stocks, bonds, etcetera), or intangible (patents, brand, etcetera). The value of tangible assets is reflected in the monetary value that they can be exchanged for.

Bonds: They are a debt that the issuer owes to the holder of the bond. Bonds are contracts that guarantee payment of a specific sum at a future date. The date that the payment of the bond's principle is due is called the maturity date. The interest rate on the principle is agreed to when the bond is initially sold. Bonds are often sold at auction, where the interest rate is set by the amount of demand for the bonds. Bonds are a common way for corporations and governments to raise funds. Municipal bonds normally have tax advantages to make them more attractive to buyers. Bonds are often resold on secondary markets. When interest rates decrease, existing bonds become more valuable since they will continue to pay the higher interest rate that they were originally sold at. Conversely, when interest rates increase, existing bonds become less valuable.

Diversification: Diversification is dividing investments among different companies, markets and types of investments. Diversification reduces risk from exposure to any one particular type of asset. Investing in various assets that react differently to market conditions reduces the overall risk and volatility.

Exchange-Traded Fund: Exchange-traded funds (ETF) hold assets, much like other types of funds. Unlike other types of funds, they are traded on stock exchanges. Exchange-traded funds generally are set up to track an index, such as the Dow Jones Industrial Average, S&P 500 or a bond index. Exchange-traded funds may also be set up to track a sector or a commodity.

Financial Advisor: This is a professional that provides advice, counsel and recommendations on financial matters. They give financial services to clients based on their client's financial situation. In many countries financial advisors are required to be trained and licensed.

Financial Risk: Financial risk is exposure to the chance of financial loss or the degree of probability of financial loss. Financial risk includes uncertainty as to the extent of financial loss. The risk could be specific to an investment, such as the risk of a company defaulting on their loan and bonds, or bankruptcy of a company. Risks can also be general risks that effect finances, such as economic down turns, war, pandemics or national collapse.

Frugal: Being frugal is reducing unnecessary consumption and avoiding waste. It requires prudent management of money to restrain spending and avoid waste. Being frugal includes resourceful use of what you already have.

Index Fund: An index fund is a mutual fund or exchange-traded fund made up of a representative sample of a group of investments with rules designed to follow certain predetermined investments, such as the Dow Jones Industrial Average, S&P 500, corporate bonds, commodity, sector, etcetera.

Instant Gratification: Instant gratification is satisfying the immediate desire even at the cost of long-term benefits. It is an inability or unwillingness to resist the temptation of an immediate reward. The desire for a smaller reward now is greater than for a larger reward later. Subjective value of rewards decreases with delay in receiving the reward. Problems with instant gratification could be related to impulse control, patience, self-control and/or willpower.

Leverage: Leverage uses debt to purchase an asset in the hope that the return on the investment will exceed the borrowing costs. Often the lender will set a limit on the amount of leverage by requiring an amount of collateral for the loan, such as 20 percent down on residential real estate or limits on the margin allowed on shares. Leverage results in greater gains when the asset increases in value. There is also risk of greater losses if the asset decreases in value. There can also be losses when the financing costs exceeds the gains from the asset.

Liabilities: Liabilities are financial obligations. They are claims on future economic benefits resulting from present or past transactions. Liabilities are payments that you are required to make in the future because of what you have done in the present or past.

Liquidity: It is the ability to quickly sell an asset without having to significantly reduce the price obtained from the asset. Liquidity is having a small trade-off between the speed of the sale and the price it can be sold for. Cash is very liquid because it can be exchanged for goods and services without any loss of value. Fixed assets, such as real estate, require significant time to sell. Liquidity would be being able to meet obligations without selling fixed assets.

Mutual Fund: Mutual funds are investment funds that pool money from many investors to purchase securities. Mutual funds are professionally managed by a company or corporation that is formed to invest the funds that it obtains, normally in diversified securities.

Net Worth: Net worth is the value of all assets owned minus the value of all outstanding liabilities. It can apply to individuals, companies or countries. It is wealth or net monetary value as expressed in terms of money or some other medium of exchange.

Opportunity Cost: It is what could have been if you had made a different choice, the loss of potential gain caused when you choose a different option, the gain that you did not receive as a result of not selecting the best option.

Return On Investment: Return on investment (ROI) is the rate of profit per unit compared to cost per unit. It is determined by using the ratio of profit divided by investment during a period of time. A common period of time is yearly, in which case return on investment would be in percent per year. The return on investment relates profits to the amount invested and can be used to compare different investments. The greater the return on investment, the better the investment performed.

Risk Tolerance: Risk tolerance is the ability to put up with the chance of loss from your investment. It is being comfortable enough to invest while knowing that there is a risk that there will be a loss from your investment. Risk tolerance is the degree of willingness to accept an uncertain payoff for the possibly of a higher payoff. It could be measured by the additional expected reward an investor requires to accept additional risk.

Stocks: Stock represents the amount of money invested in a company by buying shares in the company. Stock in a company entitles the buyer to a share of the ownership, and usually voting rights and dividends. The stock of a corporation is all of the shares that the corporation is divided into. Shares represent fractional ownership of the corporation in proportion to the total number of shares issued. Individual shares are a very small portion of the ownership of a company. Stocks are not all equal. Classes of stock may be issued with limitations on voting right or enhanced voting rights. Classes of stock may have different priority rights related to profits or the proceeds from selling the assets during bankruptcy.

Value: Value is the benefit of a good or service. It is the quality of something based on its usefulness, desirability and importance. Value is often represented monetarily by the fair market price or market return. It is the fair equivalent amount of money that a good or service is exchanged for. The value is the amount of money that someone is willing to pay for a good or service.

About the Author

I spent many years either working full time while going to school part time or going to school full time while working part time. By this process I ended up with degrees in Respiratory Therapy and Mechanical Engineering. What is more important related to this book is I have a Master's degree in Business Administration with an emphasis on finance and economics. It is not hard work alone that allowed me to have a comfortable and secure retirement; I also followed the principles of the *Formula for Wealth*.

I hope that you enjoyed this book and that it is valuable in your life. If so, please share this book with your friends and family by posting to Facebook and Twitter. I would appreciate if you could take some time to post a review on your favorite website. I wish you all the best in your future success!

~ Thank you

www.ingramcontent.com/pod-product-compliance
Lightning Source LLC
Chambersburg PA
CBHW022048050726
47591CB00002B/439